Superbike
preparation

For street and track, box stock and beyond

Jewel Hendricks

Motorbooks International
Publishers & Wholesalers Inc
Osceola, Wisconsin 54020, USA ®

First published in 1988 by Motorbooks International Publishers & Wholesalers Inc, PO Box 2, 729 Prospect Avenue, Osceola, WI 54020 USA

Printed and bound in the United States of America

Library of Congress Cataloging-in-Publication Data
Hendricks, Jewel.
     Superbike preparation: box stock and beyond/ Jewel Hendricks.
          p.   cm.
     1. Motorcycles, Racing—Design and construction.   I. Title.
TL442.H46 1988   629.2'275—dc19   88-4555 CIP
ISBN 0-87938-301-1 (pbk.)

On the cover: Yukiya Ohshima on a Suzuki (Japan) GSXR750 in the 1988 Daytona 200. *John Flory*
On the back cover: Pre-race preparation on Australian Chris Oldfield's Bimota DB1 Ducati for the 1988 Daytona 200. The author, Jewel Hendricks, with some of the tools of the trade. One of the super superbikes, a Ducati Paso 750. *Tim Parker*

For all their help on this project I'd like to give thanks to William "Slim" Jokela, Ross Kuhnle and family, C. R. Axtell, Mike Libby, Keith and Judy Code, Ron Wood, Bruce Burness, and Bob Work.
Special thanks to the patient one, Susan.

Contents

Foreword

You are about to meet an insider's insider—Jewel Hendricks—and you'll find him in Southern California.

Please notice I've specified Southern California, not southern California. The latter suggests some directional bearing along the Pacific shore, but those who live here know Southern California is a proper place, a special one, the land of enchantment in the internal-combustion world. In this land, all things are possible because all things can be built here. Need a spare or two for an SR–71 Blackbird? Fine. Some space shuttle parts? Step right up. Perhaps you need a cylinder block for a Bugatti? They know about such things here. Or one-off titanium connecting rods? Right this way.

In Southern California there are millions of machines that make other machines. Scattered through the landscape are thousands of small, highly specialized machine shops, energized by fascinating collections of engineers, artisans and craftsmen. People who live and work in such surroundings love machines. Find a person creating precision parts for the space shuttle, and you'll discover someone whose late-night passion is Lamborghinis or P51 Mustangs or racing motorcycles. At another place you might see some very curious parts, destined to go inside a Honda factory race bike—pieces that the factory engineers in Japan may only see later, if at all. In that case you could be in Jewel Hendricks' workshop.

Jewel is a member of long standing in the most inner network of motorcycle builders, engineers, artisans, theorists, fabricators, enthusiasts. When someone in this network has a question about camshafts, they don't ring up someone else who "knows about cams." They phone another one of the inner circle—a person who has spent a lifetime designing and building camshafts.

More than a decade ago my path led me to Jewel Hendricks and his magic machine tools. I was writing a story about a coachbuilt Honda 550 four. It was, among other things, a Jewel Hendricks project, and I was impressed. Hendricks . . . is a virtuoso with machine tools. He has an easy, natural understanding of machinery; almost reflexively he sees how things go together and how things can be built. It's the gift which every engineering student wishes he had, and few possess. Moreover, Hendricks works metal with such fluidity and precision that the stuff almost becomes plastic in his hands.

A lot of fancy motorcycles and R&D parts have gone through Jewel's establishment since 1975, and you are about to benefit from his experience and intelligence. He is long past that stage of trick gadgeteers who belittle what factories know and do and build; he knows the strengths of great engineering companies—and where, and why, they do less than their best in specific places. He will disappoint those who want to believe that speed comes out the end of a fancy extrusion die, or that truth lies at the center of titanium chips. But Jewel will delight those who honor virtue. He knows about intelligence and determination, patience and care.

Read Jewel well, for seldom does his private doorway to that special inside world of Southern California swing open.

Phil Schilling
Westlake Village, California

Introduction

Sport motorcycles of today are not too far from those mega-dollar factory Grand Prix machines we see in world-class events. In retrospect, I think of the many hours spent trying to make the cycles of the seventies go through a turn with aggressiveness yet without pitching the rider into the wild green. My first such encounter was on a sunny Sunday morning on the infamous racer road, Mulholland Drive, above the now-world-famous Rock Store. On my first custom-built cafe racer, trying to negotiate any sort of turn would cause the motorcycle to shake its head so violently it would mash my thumbs into the side of the gas tank. The only way to stop this was to stop the vehicle! Well, naturally I was not about to do this as there was one of those new-to-the-country Ducati Desmo 750 Super Sports on my tail and it was being ridden by the editor of *Cycle* Magazine, Cook Neilson. We proceeded past the Rock Store to a road crossing and stopped. Neilson approached me and said, "That's really a nice piece of work there, but does it handle like that all the time?" I said, "Yes, and I think I'm going to give up on it." Neilson said, "I wish I could give you some advice but I can't." Well, that was the way it was in those days.

Neilson went on to become one of the top Superbike racers in the early days of superbikes. I have to say this about Neilson, as well: he was a great advocate of the sport of motorcycling. As for me, well, I went on to make that creation of mine do what I wanted it to do.

The motorcycle that I have been describing was a Trackmaster-framed, Triumph-engined dream of mine that came about from the desire to have something different, something unique! That it was, and the lessons learned and the people it brought me in contact with were invaluable.

The motorcycle was featured on the cover of *Motorcyclist* magazine in November 1973. It was a continuing project until the day I sold it; in its final state, it sported things like a 750 cc Chantland aluminum cyl-inder, C. R. Axtell-prepared head, Allegro cams with Dell'Orto pumper carburetors, and Jack Hatley's spare Quaife five-speed, three-cylinder Triumph road racer gearbox. I rode on one of the first sets of Elliot Morris aluminum wheels with "giant" Dunlop TT100 tires.

My Triumph cafe racer featured on the cover of Motorcyclist *magazine in November 1973. When I look at this picture my mind fails to remember anyone wearing pants like those on the guy sitting on the table. Motorcyclist.*

The shocks were specially made by Bruce Burness during the early days of S&W Products. My god, I told myself, I have created the ultimate sport motorcycle! Unfortunately, on the way home from the 1974 Laguna Seca road races, I was top-ended by a stock Kawasaki 900 Z1!

That Triumph now belongs to Terry Sage and is on display in the window of his Stockton, California, motorcycle shop. Rumor has it that Kenny Roberts has visited the shop just to sit on it!

In the early- and mid-1970s, there were people out there doing things to make those motorcycles of the times go better. Anyone attending races at Laguna Seca, Ontario or Riverside would understand the term "superbike wobble parade." It was people like Pops Yoshimura and Pierre DesRoches who labored to bring those wobbly bikes into line. You had to admire riders like Yvon Duhamel, Steve McLaughlin, Reggie Pridmore, Keith "Codedog" Code and dirt tracker Dave Aldana for boarding those machines and going WFO!

In the early 1980s, performance was named Eddie Lawson, Wes Cooley and Freddie Spencer. And, with the addition of Suzuki and Honda to the programs, we said goodbye to BMWs and Ducatis as the only competitive machines.

Now we are well into the eighties with Superbike racing down to 750 cc displacement motorcycles, and names like Flying Fred Merkel, Wayne Rainey and Kevin Schwantz. This brings us to what I believe is a great format for racing—and what are these people riding? Basic off-the-floor production motorcycles. Slightly modified, of course!

Things have gotten better. We don't have to go to the extent that we used to in the good old days to make our motorcycles perform. This is not to say that we can't improve them, because we can—it's just a little less involved. Riders have a better opportunity to compete, and spectators can enjoy closer competition.

I am still a great fan of the exotic factory Grand Prix racers and the world-champion events, and was able to see the United States Grand Prix for motorcycles become a reality. You can bet that I will always be there to see all those unobtainium components that make up the Grand Prix race machine.

In order for anyone to reach the Grand Prix status, there must be a breeding ground for future riders to qualify for those exotic rides. Club racing is a good place to start, with classes for Stock Production, Superstreet, Superbike and even Grand Prix. So if you want to be just a fast sport rider, a good club racer or a world-class rider, let's consider what is involved in good motorcycle preparation.

Getting started will require being rider, tuner and sponsor. To begin with, choose a class that appeals to you and pursue it. If you intend to compete in American Motorcycle Association (AMA) events, pick a class and club that you can make points in toward qualifying for an AMA license. The Supersport class was developed by the AMA for the purpose of helping new riders get started, and it is one of the most popular and competitive classes in all clubs. The Supersport class rules limit motorcycle modifications to try and keep the expense down as much as possible. The legal modifications are just enough to make the class interesting and give the rider and tuner a good insight into setting up a racing motorcycle. These modifications are close to what I would recommend for the performance-minded street rider.

For information on rules, licensing and entries, contact the American Motorcycle Association. The address can be found in any weekly or monthly motorcycle publication.

Chapter 1

The modern motorcycle

I was once a devout Triumph fan and paid little attention to the rest of the motorcycle world. Outside of seeing the usual BSA or Norton or even an occasional Velocette, not much went on in the late 1960s and early 1970s until Kawasaki came to town in 1969 with its 500 cc triple. This was definitely the forerunner of today's pocket rocket! Before the Kawasaki 500, I had never ridden a street motorcycle that would loft the front wheel. This motorcycle was light in weight and very fast for its time. Nevertheless, I was never able to

Jeff Stern on the Team Jeff Suzuki GSXR750. I worked with the team in preparing the bike. The equipment used is apparent on the fairing: Mikuni constant velocity carbs, a Kerker Manufacturing four-into-one exhaust, Dunlop slicks and so on.

Bob Oman at Riverside Raceway on his 1972 Honda CB 750 K2. The class was for street-legal motorcycles. This bike has the modifications that were popular for the time: a Kerker pipe, double discs up front with calipers turned rearward and Akront aluminum rims with Michelin M45 PZ 2 com- pound tires. The side and center stands, along with turn signals, were removed for competition. Bob has since grown a beard to cover the scars from biting his lower lip! Jim Cook

warm up to the idea of a two-stroke motor for the street.

Kawasaki came out later with a 750 cc version which was also a fast motorcycle. These were not great-handling motorcycles, but most people of that era were not concerned with good handling. Along with the Kawasaki two-strokes was a Suzuki twin. The unique thing about these motorcycles was that the engines became the powerplants for the AMA Formula One class. They dominated the classes for a number of years when all that Yamaha had was its 350 cc water-cooled bikes. It wasn't until the appearance of the TZ700 and TZ750 race bikes that Yamaha came back. Those were great years for Formula One, with Bob Hansen's Team Green, Team Suzuki and, of course, Team Yamaha.

When I first saw the Honda CB750 four, I was sure that this machine would never become the success that it did. It was big, bulky and undoubtedly much too heavy to be a good-handling machine. My employer at the time purchased one of the first Honda 750s that came to southern California, and I got to ride it from the dealership back to work. I had trouble with the rear brake and shift lever because they operated in reverse of what I had been accustomed to. As it turned out with this and other features, the Japanese were right and other manufacturers were wrong.

The thing that impressed me about the CB750 was how fast it was for its size! A few days later, I realized that my stock 1969 Triumph Bonneville was no match for that Honda. I spent the next three years trying to make that Triumph motorcycle keep up with this new product from the land of the rising sun. As anyone knows, that Honda 750 motorcycle changed the way of thinking almost overnight. Even today I will turn to look at one of those early Honda single-cam fours, realizing what an impact they had on the motorcycle world. They don't seem to be as big as I used to picture them, either.

The Honda four quickly stimulated an aftermarket, producing a multitude of items that would transform the mighty Honda into an even higher state of

Laguna Seca, 1977. Wes Cooley on the Yoshimura-prepared Kawasaki. Check out the eyes of a gunfighter. Cycle.

Gary LaPlante is the original owner of this immaculate 1973 Kawasaki 900 Z1. The license plate reads 007 Z1, signifying that the motorcycle has number seven frame and motor. The only thing missing is the number seven packing crate that the motorcycle came in! Gary still likes to ride the Z1 on occasion, but rarely so as to keep the mileage low. Gary LaPlante

My modified Honda 550.

Early superbike: Modified Honda 550

In 1976 I bought this Honda 550 in a basket. When finished, it was a 591 cc motorcycle with not much left stock but the frame, seat, tank and engine—the engine being the most modified of the stock components.

The frame was left alone except for the insertion of tapered steering head bearings, an aftermarket swing arm made by C & J Frames and a set of Bruce Burness-tuned S & W shocks. It was the trend at that time to replace the fork tubes with Ceriani tubes and damper rods. This worked OK in the canyons but under hard breaking on the racetrack the tubes were too light. They would often distort and seize in the fork legs, causing the front end to chatter badly. In the end we went back to stock tubes with modified stock damper rods.

The engine displacement was increased by modifying Honda 750 F pistons, which had 1 mm more dome height than the Honda 750 pistons that were usually used to increase displacement.

The idea when building the engine was to use as many parts from the Honda parts department as possible. The only aftermarket parts used were S & W valve springs, Amal 28 mm concentric carburetors, an Action Fours head pipe with my own megaphone and a Lockhart oil cooler. Wheels were Morris magnesium with Michelin tires. The front brakes were stock dual Honda calipers with Hunt plasma discs attached to Honda carriers. The rear brake was a Lockheed twin-piston caliper and Lockheed rotor.

The cylinder head I did myself over a three-month period of evenings under the supervision of mentor C. R. Axtell.

All in all, this was my most rewarding motorcycle project, and the drag strip comparison showed why. The stock bike finished the quarter-mile in fifteen seconds at 76 mph. My modified bike did it in 12.03 seconds at 109.8 mph.

---

performance. How about a lightweight four-into-one exhaust system custom-made by George Kerker? The system weighed twenty-nine pounds less than stock, and the sound—well, we all recognize that sound!

Three-time Superbike champion Reggie Pridmore on the Vetter-sponsored Kawasaki at Laguna Seca, 1978. Again, the DesRoches-prepared Kawasaki was the motorcycle to beat. This particular version was the feature bike on the cover of Cycle magazine, November 1978. This was the beginning of Superbike racing as it is today. Cycle.

What was your new Honda without a new set of sticky Dunlop K81 tires mounted to newly laced Akront aluminum rims? And engine parts, double-disc kits, wheel kits and shocks? The only limits were your desire and the depth of your checkbook. That part has not changed.

Honda 750 fours started showing at the local race-tracks early on. Does anyone remember Craig Vetter on a Honda? How about Dick Mann's win at Daytona on a Honda in 1970?

During this time there were two other great Honda motorcycles, the 500 cc and 550 cc fours. After giving up on the Triumph, I bought a basket case Honda 550. I eventually modified it and it became one of the most enjoyable motorcycles that I have ever owned. The Honda 500 and 550 fours were already great-handling motorcycles and with a few minor changes they became even better—great canyon motorcycles.

The first time I met Keith "Codedog" Code was at Ontario Motor Speedway in 1973. That day he put in a very successful ride on a Honda 500 four. Bob Endicott rode a Grand Prix version Honda 500 for several years. It was the best-sounding four-cylinder of the time; you always knew where Bob was on the racetrack just by the sound.

About the time the Honda four had reached its full state of development, what should come along but the incredible Kawasaki Z1! It was a 900 cc motorcycle with—what did you say?—dual overhead camshafts.

My modified Kawasaki KZ1000.

Early superbike: Modified Kawasaki KZ1000

Eddie Lawson won the Superbike National at Laguna Seca in 1979 on what appeared to be a stock-bodied Kawasaki MK11. Well, at least the *body work* was stock.

This idea stimulated my interest in building a new motorcycle for the street. I started with a bent Z1R frame from a guy in Santa Barbara, California, and a practically new Z1R engine from a junkyard in Chatsworth, California. With the help of Pierre DesRoches and a trip to Craig Vetter's place in San Luis Obispo, we discovered the whereabouts of all the body work that was left over from one of Vetter's Kawasaki projects, found at the Kawasaki shop in San Luis Obispo. I purchased three complete sets of body parts and many other hard-to-find items for my new project.

Many months, many hours and many dollars later, the Kawasaki was finished. It boasted a cylinder head with J-model valves, Moriwaki cams and followers, 31 mm Mikuni smooth bore carburetors and Moriwaki 1105 pistons. Also included were a completely modified cam chain idler and adjustment system, Bassani exhaust system and Lockhart oil cooler. The shocks were custom tailored by Bruce Burness of Ohlins. The brakes were Lockheed with discs from a Yamaha OW31 750 cc road racer bolted to one of the last sets of Morris magnesium wheels to be produced.

The Kawasaki had its day on the Kerker dyno, and the aftermarket ignition system literally came apart. Even so, the engine managed to make 104 hp at 8500 rpm—not too bad for a 1980 street machine. The ignition was replaced with a complete 1980 Kawasaki J-model system and has run happily ever after.

Daytona, 1977. Left to right: Keith Code, Lyn Abrams and Pierre DesRoches. Abrams, founder and owner of Racecrafters, was also a partner in the ownership of Kerker Manufacturing with DesRoches. Code went on to form the successful California Superbike School.

Why in the world would you need two camshafts? Like the Honda four, the Kawasaki 900 Z1 became a very popular motorcycle, and it did not take long for the Z1 to take its place at the top of the performance

scale—with aftermarket performance components to boot.

But the Z1, as anyone who ever owned one will testify, had an inherent handling problem. It liked to shake its head while the rider was trying to get through high-speed turns. This problem seemed to get even worse the more the motorcycle was modified. Pierre DesRoches, who then owned part of Kerker Manufacturing, came up with a good cure for the local street riders by installing Kawasaki 650 cc triple clamps. This gave the motorcycle a little more trail. A set of S&W aftermarket shocks on the rear helped ease the problem a bit more. Most production motorcycles are set up for riding two people, which makes them a little stiff for one person. Making the Z1 really handle became a major project.

The Ducati Super Sport made its appearance during this time. The early Superbike class saw some close competition between three manufacturers and the racing was great. I remember a Riverside AMA National when at any spot on the track you could have thrown a blanket over Reggie Pridmore on his BMW, Cook Neilson on his Ducati and Steve McLaughlin straddling his Kawasaki. For a whole season these guys were the show to watch in Superbike racing.

A year or two later Pierre DesRoches, sponsored by Racecrafters, was preparing Kawasakis for Reggie Pridmore to compete in the AMA-sanctioned Superbike events. The frames had to be highly modified, the head angle was changed and the headstock was lowered by 0.75 in. to increase ground clearance. Tapered steering head bearings were installed. Other braces

Daytona, 1977. Keith Code on the Racecrafters-sponsored Kawasaki gridding for the Superbike final. Notice the stock exhaust system on the motorcycles; the class was aimed more toward production racing in the early days.

Cook Neilson lining up for a late afternoon final at Ontario Speedway on Old Blue, as the Ducati 900 SS became affectionately known. The person in motion to the left is the current editor of Cycle, Phil Schilling. Along with his duties at Cycle, Schilling has somehow always found the time over the years to continue tuning motorcycles—and somehow all those motorcycles were very fast!

and gussets were welded into the frame to make it stiffer. Heavy aluminum motor mount plates were used to make the engine act as a frame member. The swing arm legs were split and a metal shear strip was welded in. The welds were smoothed by hand and repainted to look stock (of course it was against the rules). I was involved with DesRoches on some of the modifications to those race bikes and believe me, it was a lot of work. Many hours were spent on the flow bench and dyno at C. R. Axtell's facility in Sun Valley, California. The results paid off. Pridmore and DesRoches won the 1977 and 1978 AMA Superbike championships.

Suzuki Motor Company did not stand still during this time. Its GS750 and GS1000 became popular, and rightfully so. The engines were great, the motorcycles looked good and were great-handling machines. Suzuki advocated owner maintenance by making available workshop manuals, special tools and, of course, parts. It was Suzuki's turn to dominate the market— and the Superbike class.

Honda got involved again on the factory level and sported the largest and flashiest teams, as only Honda can do. Even with the financial cutbacks for 1988 they

My friend, the infamous, illusive and always humorous Travis Bean with his personalized (Old Shep) Suzuki GS1000. To this day the bike is still ridden to and from work. Of the motorcycles in Bean's stable this one will probably never be sold simply because it's the one that his wife, Rita, likes to ride with him on.

In 1979 I purchased this Suzuki GS750ES with the intent to leave it alone and just ride it. Instead I drilled the discs, front and rear. And I installed a chrome Kerker pipe. Yes, those are 29 mm smooth bore Mikuni carburetors and, yes, the motorcycle was used as a test vehicle for the development of Ohlins street shocks. Oh yes, those are Kawasaki turn sig-

nals. The Suzuki GS850 gas tank did give one more gallon of fuel capacity for those long rides, and I did repaint with International School Bus Racing Yellow! I logged 27,000 miles on this motorcycle in two years. It was the sports touring fever time for me and just another great motorcycle.

Reggie Pridmore and tuner Pierre DesRoches at Daytona in 1977 on the Racecrafters-sponsored Kawasaki. Cycle.

The legendary Pops Yoshimura doing some cam timing. I can't think of anyone who has had a greater influence on the sport of Superbike racing than Pops. Dave Wolman.

are still the team to beat in AMA Superbike racing.

I have enjoyed the racing events over the years, watching the riders and machines of Honda, Kawasaki, Suzuki and Yamaha compete against one another. For me there is no other motorsport quite like motorcycle racing.

As the years pass, so do last year's motorcycle models. What do they now hold in store? Street-legal, DOT-approved Grand Prix road racers! Step right up, folks. Pick your paint and decals, because they're all great!

Last year's 1000 cc cycles are out-performed by this year's 750 cc motorcycles. This represents several things. The engines are in a higher state of tune. The overall weight of the vehicle is down. They are liquid cooled. Wheels and tires are wider, larger and lighter. Brakes are bigger and better. The bikes handle like never before, and surrounding all this is a complete set of Grand Prix body work!

The aluminum frame has come into vogue, as well as what I believe to be the single most important advancement in the motorcycle sport over the years—electronic ignition.

Having been involved in motorcycling for some time now, I have pretty much established a direction for myself of competitive posing and profiling, along with some occasional sports touring. I enjoy working with young people, particularly with those who wish to go racing. The questions are the same; young people are just more energetic about it.

What's a good motorcycle to buy? That is a difficult question. I may answer by asking, what are you going to do with it and how much money can you spend? Most of the time I get the feeling that it wasn't what they wanted to hear, but it's something that should be thought about carefully, unless you can afford to buy and try one of each! I think it is important to choose a machine that is appealing, whether it be old or new, large displacement or small, cruiser, sport or racer. For high performance, four valves per cylinder and liquid cooling is a must. Availability of performance parts must be considered. Keep an eye and ear open for new models that may make your purchase outdated almost overnight, particularly if the motorcycle will be used for racing.

Most of all, I highly recommend everyone to buy and ride the motorcycle of your choice. Do it wisely and safely. Ride alone or with a group. Race if you wish. Participate in the sport, and I guarantee it will be enjoyable!

Chapter 2

Basic geometry

There are five principles in motorcycle geometry that I would like to cover: head angle or rake; trail or caster; wheelbase; center of gravity; and anti-squat.

If you were to turn to engineering journals on these subjects, you would be deluged with mathematical formulas that would require a degree from a techni-

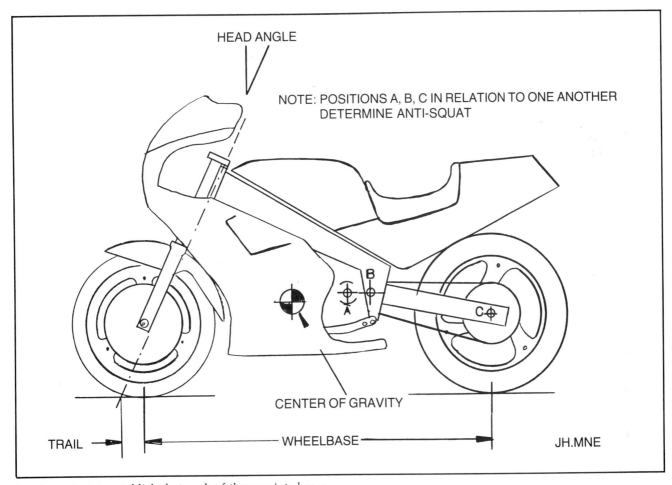

HEAD ANGLE

NOTE: POSITIONS A, B, C IN RELATION TO ONE ANOTHER DETERMINE ANTI-SQUAT

B
A
C

CENTER OF GRAVITY

TRAIL — WHEELBASE — JH.MNE

It is important to establish that each of these points has a definite relationship to one another. If one is changed, all others are affected.

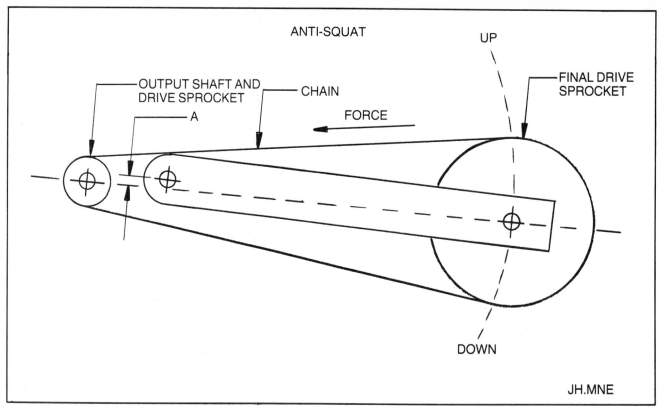

*The placement of the swing arm pivot in relation to the line through the center of the output shaft and the center of the rear axle establishes a neutral, squat or anti-squat situation in the swing arm geometry. Placing the swing arm pivot too high above the line will lead to an anti-squat situation or the forcing of the rear wheel to the road surface under hard acceleration. If the swing arm pivot is placed too low this can produce a squat situation or the lifting of the rear wheel off the road surface under hard acceleration. The ideal place-*ment will allow the swing arm to pivot freely under hard acceleration. Most motorcycle pivot arms are placed properly. If changing the ride height by shortening or lengthening the shock length, keep in mind the effect it may have on how the swing arm functions during hard acceleration. If dimension A on this diagram is too high the swing arm will be forced down under power. If dimension A is too low the swing arm will be forced up. If things are properly set the swing arm can move freely during acceleration and braking.*

cal school to understand. For the sake of simplicity, let's assume that the motorcycle manufacturers with their computerized engineering departments have taken care of the details and left the enthusiast with a product that incorporates the above principles in the right places, needing only minor tuning for special applications.

First let me explain in plain language these five principles of geometry and the effect they have on our motorcycles.

Steering head angle or rake allows us to turn the motorcycle by placing the tire contact patch to the left or right of the line of the vehicle as the front wheel is turned. Head angle is determined by the angle from perpendicular that the headstock is built into the motorcycle frame.

Trail or caster keeps the wheel centered in the direction of travel. The combination of more rake and trail will make the motorcycle more stable in a straight line, but will require more effort from the rider to negotiate turns. Less rake and trail will make the motorcycle more responsive or sensitive but may affect the overall stability at higher speeds.

Trail has been increasing from the standard a few years ago of about 3.375 to more than four inches. Currently, the trail on popular sport motorcycles seems to be back to around 3.375 in. Oversensitive, unstable steering can lead to that ever unpopular wobble or tank slapper syndrome if the motorcycle front end becomes light under hard acceleration or when cresting a rise in the road surface.

Wheelbase is the dimension between front and rear axle. Shorter wheelbases increase quickness in handling and are dictated by engine placement, radiators, monoshocks and other components that make up the motorcycle.

Center of gravity is the point where the motorcycle, if suspended, would balance evenly whether on its side, rightside up or upside down. This point again is established by the placement of the components that make up the motorcycle.

Anti-squat is the dynamic force in the rear suspension that can add to or subtract from the downforce at the point at which the tire contacts the ground.

The placement of the swing arm pivot in relation to the line through the center of the output shaft and the center of the rear axle establishes the anti-squat situation in the swing arm geometry. Placing the swing arm pivot too high above the line can lead to a situation that will put too much force on the rear wheel to the road surface under hard acceleration, lifting the rear of the motorcycle and locking the suspension. If the swing arm pivot is placed too low this can cause the rear wheel to lift away from the road surface under hard acceleration. The ideal placement will allow the swing arm to pivot freely under hard acceleration.

Most swing arm pivot points are well placed. If changing the ride height by shortening or lengthening the shock, keep in mind the effect it may have on tire traction and suspension movement during hard acceleration.

Keep in mind that the engineering departments of major motorcycle manufacturers have gone to great lengths to put all these principles together to produce a high-performance vehicle. The modification of any one of these areas will have an effect on all the others;

keep this in mind also when making changes or modifications to any of the five principles listed. These areas can be tuned for maximum performance. Tuning is refining, and refining means minute changes.

Once these five principles are tuned in you would think they would remain constant, but under hard acceleration or under hard braking in particular, everything changes. The forks compress. The rake and trail lessens. The center of gravity changes and the wheelbase shortens. With all these sudden changes you would think that the handling would decrease, but an interesting thing happens: with weight transfer forward during hard braking nearing 100 percent, the contact patch of the front tire from the increased load becomes larger and shifts rearward, creating a situation that keeps the front tire centered in the direction of travel. All things being correct, the motorcycle maintains stability during the effects of hard braking.

To offset some of the effects of hard braking, anti-dive systems have become common on performance motorcycles. Anti-dive is a system that simply allows the external adjustment of the compression damping

In the background is a Ducati 750 Sport. This motorcycle was noted for its high-speed stability. It is interesting to note the visual difference in the head angle to that of the more current Suzuki GSXR750 which is considered to be a very good handling motorcycle, to say the least. The Suzuki in order to support its shallow head angle has a shorter wheelbase. More weight on the front wheel and more trail add up to better low-speed handling without sacrificing high-speed handling and stability.

orifices, which slow down the front end's tendency to dive under hard braking. Some are mechanically controlled, such as on Hondas. Some are electrically controlled, such as on the Suzuki GSXR1100. When not being applied under hard braking, the damping returns to normal, giving back smoother ride quality. The rake and trail is also retained by the anti-dive system's not allowing the front forks to compress as rapidly as forks without anti-dive.

Another important factor to consider in a high-performance motorcycle is its ability, under hard braking, to keep a good line while in a turn. Some motorcycles have a tendency to rise up and straighten out in a turn with the brakes still on. Some of this is acceptable, but not in excess.

Hard braking has another extreme effect on geometry in that it renders the rear tire and brake almost useless. In the case of the rear brake, who cares? But if the rear tire contact is lost—well can you imagine?

Wheelbase and center of gravity are dictated by the placement of components that make up the motor-cycle: wheel and tire sizes; engine size and shape; radiators and shocks; and other parts necessary for a complete vehicle.

The swing arm placement is an important part of the overall geometry of the motorcycle. What seems to be just a horizontal forked member that holds the rear is actually a much more important component. The length is determined by wheel size, tire size and the area that is needed for the pivot. Swing arms have become longer because of the necessity to mount components for single-shock applications. With higher demands for handling, swing arms must be larger in section to handle extra loads.

The placement of the swing arm pivot in the frame in relation to the output shaft and the rear axle is important. This will determine anti-squat effects on the motorcycle under hard acceleration. If for instance the swing arm pivot is too low, under hard acceleration the power transmitted by the chain will tend to lift the wheel off the ground. This is not a condition you want to have happen while leaned hard over exiting a turn.

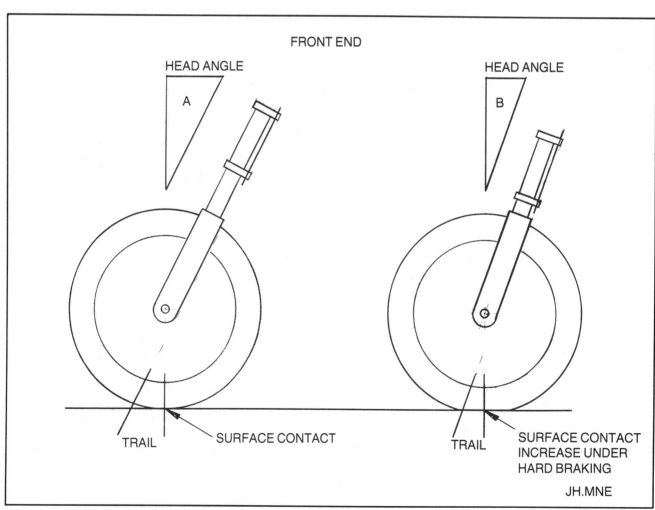

This drawing shows the difference between static position of a motorcycle front end and the position under hard braking. Under hard braking the forks compress reducing the head angle (rake) and trail. This would lead one to believe that with reduced rake and trail stability would also be reduced, but during hard braking the transfer of weight forward causes the contact patch of the front tire to increase and therefore maintain stability.

On the other hand, having the swing arm pivot too high would cause the swing arm to be pulled down with too much force, tying up the suspension—also undesirable. These are important things to consider when changing the ride height of a motorcycle where the swing arm pivot position has already been determined.

Motorcycle manufacturers have done a great job with new designs. We, the enthusiastic consumers, enjoy great-handling motorcycles today because of their designs. Therefore I don't recommend making major changes to today's performance motorcycle geometry, but there can be some good tuning in these areas.

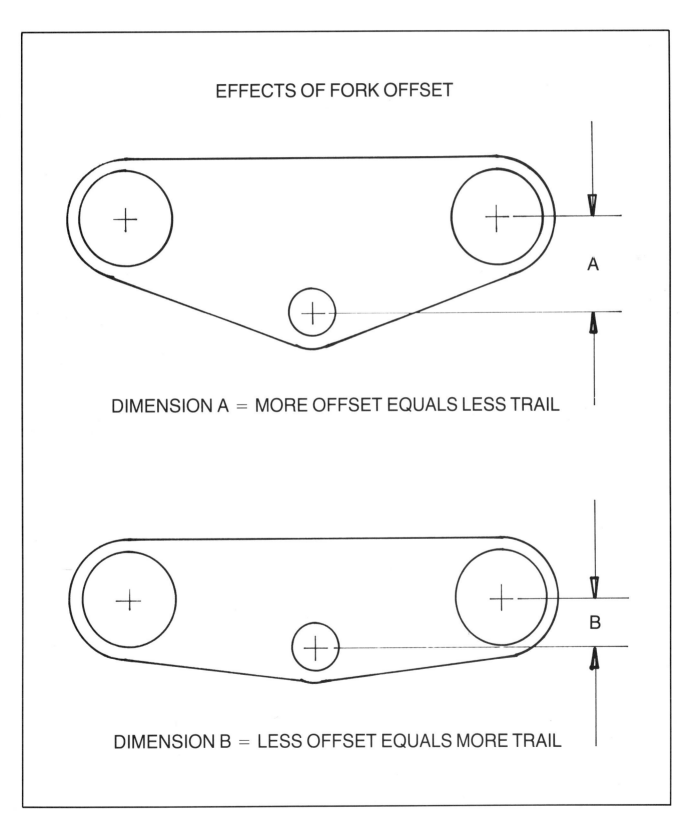

EFFECTS OF FORK OFFSET

DIMENSION A = MORE OFFSET EQUALS LESS TRAIL

DIMENSION B = LESS OFFSET EQUALS MORE TRAIL

Chapter 3

The chassis

When I think of the motorcycle frame, I think first of the Norton Manx and Irishman Rex McCandless who designed the Featherbed frame. On its first public appearance in 1950 the Featherbed, powered by a 500 cc Norton single, won its race with Geoff Duke riding.

The Featherbed's design was straightforward. Large-diameter lightweight steel duplex tubes started at the steering head and went down and around the engine, bending back over the top and returning to the steering head with one length of tubing per side. The design at the steering head featured multiple triangulation for strength and rigidity, and the frame incorporated a swing arm with suspension units. An idea that McCandless developed around 1946, it was a very innovative concept for that time. Most of these ideas for a

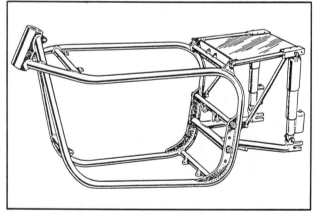

The Featherbed frame was designed by Irishman Rex Mc-Candless and was first used on Norton racers way back in 1950. The most innovative thing about the Featherbed was the swing arm using two suspension units from an automobile. Suspension units were later designed specifically for the Featherbed frame. Riding on this frame was described by works rider Harold Daniell as like sleeping on a feather bed, thus establishing its name.

different type of motorcycle frame all added up to a better-handling motorcycle.

McCandless went to work for Norton and with his employment went any claim to the Featherbed frame design. The racing success that Norton achieved in the fifties speaks well of the McCandless design. The frame became popular with street riders who installed about every engine available at the time for that individual touch. The Featherbed frame has had such an influence on the motorcycle industry to the present day. Hardly a motorcycle frame built today does not use at least some of the design parameters set by Rex McCandless for the Featherbed frame.

There have been other successful frame designs over the years such as the single backbone, the triangulated space frame (Bimota), the monocoque, the perimeter and so on. The single most amazing thing about motorcycle frames, however, is that they are all designed to do the same thing.

The present trend is the aluminum frame with extruded rectangular members traveling alongside the engine welded to extruded, forged or cast headstocks and swing arm pivot members. The cradle portion of the frame is bolted to one side so the engine can be removed. The swing arm is made of large-section aluminum-box extrusions welded to cast or extruded members. Some swing arms are completely cast (Honda Interceptor '83–84). The Yamaha Delta Box frame uses formed sheet metal sides welded to Yamaha headtube casting and swing arm pivot members.

Are these aluminum frames the answer? They are nice looking and they do seem to work, but some motorcycle manufacturers are still using steel frames while others are going back to steel frames after offering aluminum in past years. One thing is certain: whatever you have for a machine now is going to work well.

The Norton Manx with its duplex loop frame and swing arm with twin suspension units. This system set the trend for motorcycle frames for many years and its influence is still evi- dent. A classic example of function is form. Even by today's standards it is a beautiful motorcycle.

The FZR750 and FZR1000 frames are formed aluminum sheet members welded to casting with square steel cradles bolted to the underside of the engine. Very nicely done. The frame is one of those that needs no bracing.

The Yamaha FZR frame curves very nicely around the wide bank of four carburetors. Even the welding is attractive.

A frame must be in good alignment for it to function as designed, however. All industries have what is called production tolerances, which are simply areas plus or minus the dimension callout of a particular part or structure on a blueprint. For example, a headstock is to be installed at 26 1/2 degrees plus or minus one-half degree, meaning the headstock must be welded in at twenty-six to twenty-seven degrees in order to pass inspection. When a frame is being sent to the frame shop, you want to align it as close to the manufacturer's callout as possible, eliminating those plus or minus figures. In other words, blueprint it.

The two most important points on the frame are the angle of the headstock, its center and its relation to the swing arm axis. Other points on the frame such as motor mounts and component attachment areas can now be checked. It is a good idea to have the engine cases in the frame when it is aligned, as it serves as a frame member.

The swing arm now goes through the same process making sure that the pivot bosses are parallel with the rear axle. The centerline of the swing arm should be established so that the legs of the swing arm can be aligned to the motorcycle centerline. This will place a correctly spaced rear wheel in a proper line with the front wheel.

Before taking a frame for alignment, check with the manufacturer for its specific requirements. It will instruct you on how the frame should be presented.

Gusseting and reinforcing is almost a thing of the past with today's frames, but I will give a few examples of what is being done. Today, the GSXR750 Suzuki is the most popular performance street motorcycle and also the most popular racetrack motorcycle. For the street, the aluminum frame is more than sufficient. For the racetrack, it can stand a little reinforcement.

Swing arms

The swing arm on most modern motorcycles can use some attention. For street use I don't recommend any modification. As for production racing, most racing association rule books don't allow it. Superbike and Superstreet classes allow these modifications, however. These classes also allow engine modifications along with slick racing tires; these changes will put more stress on a frame and swing arm.

Building a complete swing arm assembly was popular a few years ago with a few companies supplying aftermarket swing arms. CalFab, a southern Cali-

The Italian Bimota is true motorcycle art. Here are two SB4s. The one in the foreground has the SB4 stock Suzuki GS1100 motor. The one in the background has been highly modified and the GS1100 powerplant was bored to 1340 cc. The frame construction is what is called triangulated—each section of the frame forming a triangle. The overall frame is light and very rigid, but costly to produce. I deserve to own one someday!

My hand-built Kreidler 50 cc road racer. The German water-cooled rotary valve engine makes 16.5 hp at 17,000 rpm. Details included a 32 mm Bing carb, six-speed gearbox, Brembo calipers and discs, Campagnolo wheels with Michelin tires and a dry clutch. The bike weighed in at 118 lb. wet. I used a single large-diameter tube for the main frame support. The idea came from the frames used in dirt track racing at the time, 1977. What was it like to ride? Very stable. You can get the same feeling by going about 100 mph on a ten-speed bicycle. I won the 1977–78 season championship for 50 cc bikes with this.

Typically beautiful work by Ron Wood on his prototype 500 cc road racing motorcycle. Later in the season it would be modified for a monoshock rear suspension system. Com- *plete with new seat, tank and fairing, it was an impressive piece of work.*

fornia company, will still build custom swing arms for almost any model of motorcycle. It also makes and installs a nice reinforcement that I think is worth considering if the motorcycle is to be raced in classes that allow such modifications.

When all modifications have been completed to the frame and swing arm, it is ready for alignment. If the frame you are taking for alignment has been crashed, you might like to take along the triple clamps and fork tubes and have them checked. A slightly bent front end can be hard to detect without the proper measuring equipment.

When reassembling the frame it is important to set the steering head bearing races with a driver or punch.

The Wood–Rotax 500 Grand Prix racer in full trim. The motorcycle is being developed to compete in Formula II road *racing events. The motorcycle is an immaculate creation, typical of anything done by Ron Wood.*

See your service manual for details. Normally the races are removed for aligning.

When put back together, the swing arm should have no noticeable side-to-side play (endplay). Nor should the swing arm have any great resistance when it is moved on its pivotal arc. Close attention to the swing arm pivot axle torque figure is important when assembling.

Another important area of assembly is the triple clamps. Pay close attention to the data in the service manual, particularly the torque figures on the spanner nuts and top crown nut. The manufacturer has established this data for good reason. Overtorquing will make short life of the steering head bearings. Under-

Every bit helps. Thicker motor mount plates were added to this GSXR750. These plates are fabricated after the frame has been aligned, and can be custom-fitted to the frame without changing the frame position. The bolt holes are reamed for a better fit. To transfer the hole patterns, a set of transfer pins are machined. The punch marks are picked up on the milling machine for a precision placement of the motor mount plate holes.

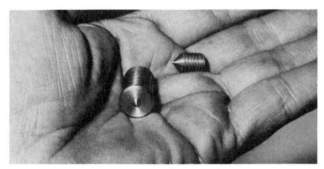

Machined transfer pins used for marking the precision center of holes in a motor mount plate.

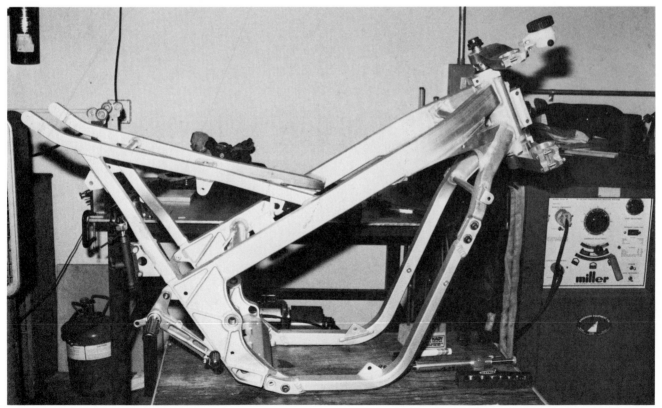

Yamaha RZV500 aluminum frame in the shop for modifications to the foot peg placement and remounting of a Brembo rear master cylinder. Notice custom-made triple clamps and remote front brake master cylinder reservoir.

Changing the footpeg position to meet the requirements of the rider means fabrication of new aluminum brackets. The stock rear master cylinder is being replaced on this frame. Relocating the footpegs may have an influence on placement of the master cylinder. This is a Yamaha RZV500.

Rear axle mounting and adjusting methods

Over the years, an area that has always interested me is the methods used by manufacturers to hold and adjust the rear axle. For a while, there was the eccentric method, Kawasaki's. Now there is the popular box section with inner sliding block. It works all right and is cost-effective. The most commonly used system, however, is what I call the flat plate with clevis adjuster. No matter what style hits the street models for the year, you have only to look to the racing scene to see what is probably the best method used, particularly among the factory teams. A flat plate with clevis adjuster is currently the trick: this applies to the old philosophy that when they get it right, they will all look the same!

The flat plate with clevis adjuster is the simplest and most efficient method of mounting the rear wheel to the swing arm. Well, almost. On its mono swing arm endurance racers, Honda has gone back to the eccentric method of chain adjustment. I don't mind that, considering how easy it is to remove the rear wheel!

Steering head bearings

Certain motorcycle models come equipped with tapered roller bearings, and there is no doubt as to the tapered bearing's superiority. One of the selling points

torquing means a loose front end; at speed it could ruin your day. Remember, the front wheel axle, the steering stem, the swing arm pivot and the rear wheel axle tied into the frame keep this motorcycle together as a unit.

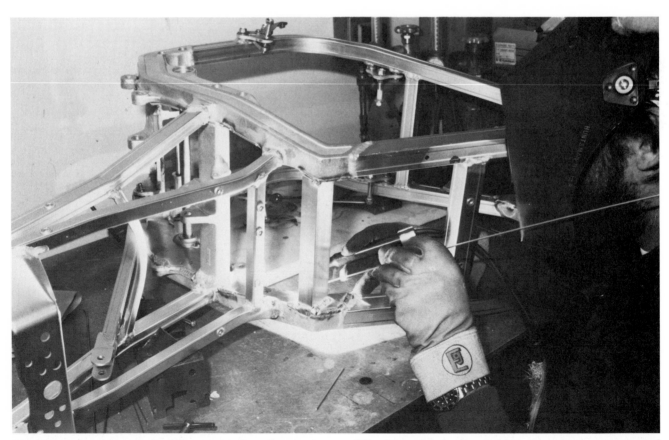

Once all the gusseting and reinforcements have been cut and fitted, they are welded into place with a heli-arc welder. It is very important to have the frame in clean condition and the anodized finish removed in the area of the welds as it is difficult to weld aluminum that is in any way contaminated with oil, grease, paint or anodized metal. This is a Suzuki GSXR750 frame.

of the 1983 Honda VF750 Interceptor was the fact that it came with tapered roller bearings in the headstock. But you won't find this type of bearing in later-model Hondas such as the 1000 Interceptor, Hurricane 600 cc or 1000 cc. Why? They have been replaced by more cost-effective ball bearings—at about half the price.

I did a little research at my local Honda parts department and found that the tapered bearings that came stock in the 1983 VF750 Interceptor would also fit in the headstock bores of a 1984 VF1000F that I was rebuilding. What a nice little update for my project. My point is to do a little research in an area that might lead to an improvement. Tapered steering head bearings are a definite improvement over ball bearings.

Another view of the stiffer Suzuki GSXR750 frame.

When gusseting has to follow a curve, it is progressively clamped and tack-welded into place. This is a Suzuki GSXR750 frame.

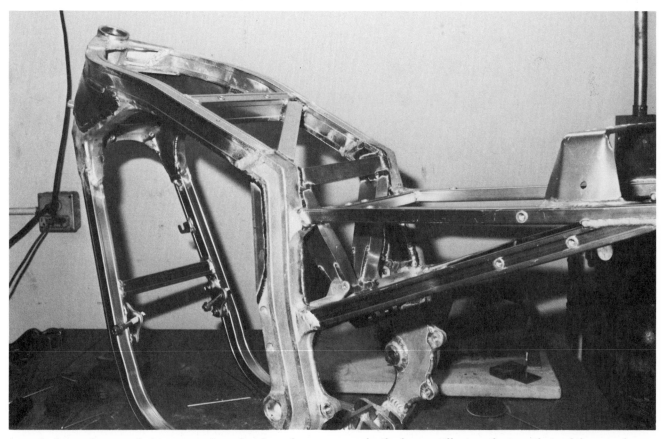

A total of ten plates and six rectangular tubes have been welded into this Suzuki GSXR750 frame. The purpose is to make the frame stiffer in order to withstand the extra horsepower and demands required in road race competition.

Sheet aluminum plates have been pop-riveted to the frame sides of this nicely prepared Vance & Hines Suzuki GSXR750. Vance & Hines made their name in Pro-Stock drag racing, but have branched out into road racing.

This 1984 Honda VF1000F frame is ready to go for straightening. The engine cases have been bolted into all mounting points. The swing arm is in place and the steering head races have been removed. The triple clamps and fork tubes should be included so they may be checked as well. It is also a good idea to include the rear wheel—in place.

Steering damper

I highly recommend the use of a steering damper. I have been in a few situations where, had I had a steering damper or had the one on my motorcycle been properly adjusted, I would not have experienced the physical and emotional pain that I did.

A nice example of an aftermarket swing arm with gusseting and bracing included. Work was done by CalFab, a company that specializes in this type of work. This unit is to be fitted to a Yamaha YZR500 aluminum frame.

The Yoshimura GSXR1100 with the swing arm bracing on the underside. The stock rear axle adjustment has been kept, but the slot in the swing arm has been elongated allowing for additional adjustment if needed, and not just for chain adjustment, but so that the wheelbase can be changed to suit course.

The swing arm on Dr. John Wittner's winning Moto Guzzi shows some well-thought-out bracing done in steel. This whole motorcycle is a marvel of ingenuity in both machining and fabrication. I would even let Dr. John work on my teeth! This motorcycle, with Doug Brauneck aboard, won the 1987 AMA Pro-Twins season championship.

A complete aftermarket swing arm on a Vance & Hines street-legal GSXR. Notice the different rear axle mounting and adjusting method used. The different axle mounting and swing arm bracing afford more rigidity to the overall frame unit.

The rear axle adjusting system on Wayne Rainey's works Honda VFR750. If Honda uses this style of rear axle mounting and adjustment, you have to accept the fact that it works.

With the power available on today's sportbikes it's very easy to make the front end lighter. A front end needs a certain amount of weight to function as designed, however, and without this weight the front end is free to do what it wants. I guarantee that once it starts that oscillation known as a "tank slapper," you will wish you had a steering damper!

For racing, along with the installation of a steering damper, the forkstops should be modified to cut the travel to within the rules of the racing association that is competed in. (The AMA rule specifies fifteen degrees left to right from center.)

In selecting a steering damper I recommend only the adjustable style. There are kits available that will make the installation easier.

Tapered bearings are by far superior to ball bearings for use in the steering head. They are also more expensive. The bearings in the photo are used in a number of Honda motorcycles, both dirt and street. These are the same part number as for the 1983 VF750, and can be installed in a 1984 VF1000F which came standard with ball bearings. If your motorcycle does not come with taper bearings, check with your local parts store to see what's available.

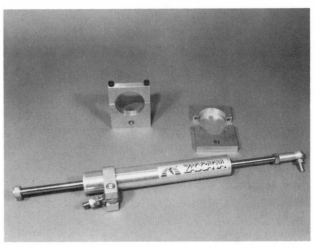

Zaccaria steering damper. I rough out the damper mounts and then, depending on the fork application, I bore and finish the part. There are a number of steering dampers available; here is one of the better quality units. Something to check on a steering damper is that at its centered position there is no free play in the damping action.

A steering damper for the street is a good idea; in a race situation it is a must. There are a number of brands available, but whatever brand is chosen, be sure to check for any play in the valving by positioning the shaft at the midpoint in the body. There should be no free play in the damping at this point. This is a Bimota SB4 with Suzuki GS1100 motor.

An HRC steering damper on a Honda 600 Hurricane, complete with lightened and drilled titanium mounting bolt.

One of the little things that helped Doug Polen win the 1987 AMA Supersport class championship.

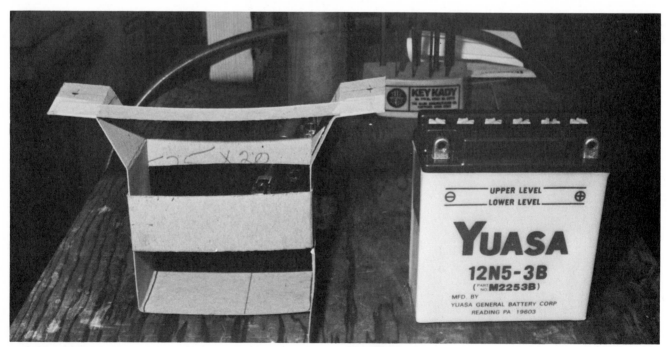

A racing application does not require the battery that a street motorcycle does, so fabrication of a battery box to house a smaller battery was a weight and space saving change. Using cardboard and some tape, a mockup is made first from a cardboard box. Using the mockup for a pattern, the actual parts are cut from 1/8 inch aluminum sheet and welded together. The smaller battery gives space for the oil catch tank on this Suzuki GSXR750 superbike.

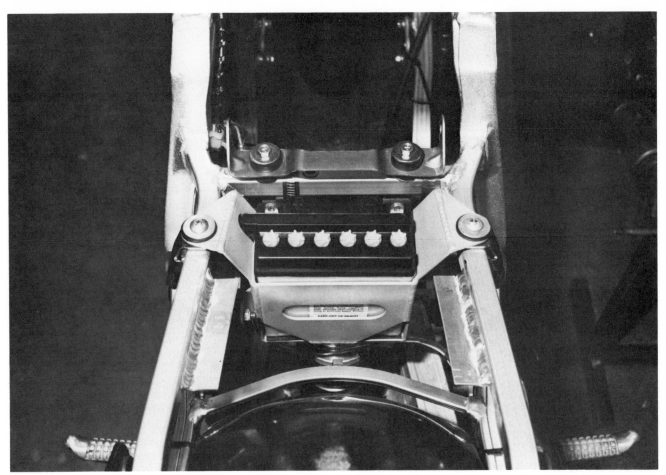

The finished battery box in place gives the frame a well-prepared look. This is a Suzuki GSXR750.

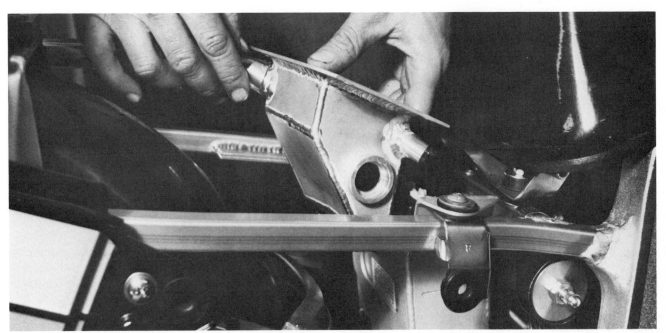

Racing associations will require oil and water catch tanks on the motorcycle in order to compete. Photo shows a fabricated aluminum catch tank for a GSXR750. The large hole in the lower corner is for a sight window. At high rpm an engine can "wet sump" or create enough pressure in the crankcase to blow oil out the oil vent tube. Anyone who has ever been oiled down will understand the value of an oil or water catch tank which—if properly designed—will keep oil or water from reaching the atmosphere.

Chapter 4

Wheels, tires and brakes

The Metzeler ME 1 Comp K and Lazer mounted on the rear of Cal Rayborn's FZR1000. This is still a good choice for performance street tires.

Wheels

Spoked wheels had their day some years ago when drum brakes were all that was available in the world of motorcycles. I remember Elliot Morris, the person who gave us the magnesium motorcycle wheel here in the United States. Morris was a very enthusiastic person who wanted to develop something really useful for the motorcycle aftermarket and particularly the racer. Morris was a perfectionist in the finest form, and he was concerned with the safety of riders using his product both on the street and track. Morris believed in the concept of tubeless tires and wider rims for motorcycles, and went round and round with tire manufacturers over the issue. I think he was finally convincing.

The first racing wheels that Morris made were used on Team Hansen Kawasakis. Triumph began using them on its three-cylinder road racers along with Yamaha on its 250 cc and 350 cc machines, and later on the Formula 750 class machines. After the class for Superbikes was established in the 1970s, hardly a motorcycle on the grid at any event in the country was equipped with anything but Morris magnesium wheels. The Morris wheel became the standard for racers and street riders of the time. Even today you have just to look around to see the influence that this man had on the modern motorcycle wheel.

Aside from being wide, light and handsome, the magnesium and aluminum wheel had other benefits. It allowed the fitting of disc brakes with opposed-piston calipers. Until this time we had to live with single-piston calipers because it was difficult to make a spoked hub narrow enough to allow a caliper with a piston on the inside. Lockheed calipers and discs were available in those days but hard to install on spoked wheels. The Morris wheel allowed for the needed space.

Many of today's motorcycles, race and street, come standard with the best wheels and brakes available. In most cases there is no need to update at all. Aftermarket wheel suppliers like EPM and Campagnolo have discontinued manufacturing wheels. About all that is used today are the three-spoke Marvic, the Dymag and the Yoshimura, supplied by Technomechanica. The 1987 Yamaha FZR750 and FZR1000 came standard with Marvic-style wheels cast in aluminum. In 1987 the Honda CBR line was fitted with a unique S-style three-spoke wheel also cast in aluminum. In 1985, Suzuki GSXRs were equipped with the first really lightweight aluminum wheel for production motorcycles. Honda followed in 1986 with a Dymag style on the VFR, and supplies a unique six-spoke wheel for its superbikes and Grand Prix racers.

The lightweight aluminum wheel for the street machine is the better choice. Aluminum is stronger and much more resistant to the effects of corrosion and abuse. As for replacement, they are more readily available and the cost is considerably less than for aftermarket wheels. The widths of production wheels are well matched to tires that are currently available.

If you have any doubt as to the performance level of today's production motorcycles, just take a trip to your local club race some weekend and notice how fast some riders are going on production wheels (with DOT tires mounted, of course).

If, on the other hand, you are planning to compete in the Superstreet or Superbike classes, then magnesium wheels are a real consideration not just for the weight savings but because of tire choice. Slick tires are allowed in these classes and require wider rim widths. Wider rims are a must with the coming of the radial tire to the motorcycle world. Check with tire manufacturers for specifications or see what is being used at the local racetrack.

Wheel bearings

In all the miles that I have traveled on a motorcycle, I have never had a wheel bearing failure. I have heard of and seen wheel bearing failure, however. Someone came to my shop one day with a rear wheel bearing failure, his story being that the bearing went out almost immediately after installing a new bearing. I agreed to look at the situation and discovered that the inner spacer was gone. The inner spacer is a piece of tubing with a dimension that is critical.

Motorcycle wheel bearings are usually of the ball type which can withstand high radial loads. Ball bearings are also designed to withstand some thrust load or

The Metzeler ME 1 Comp K and Lazer mounted on the front of Cal Rayborn's FZR1000.

side loading. Without the inner spacer, the torque of the axle nut forces the ball of the bearing against the side of the bearing races with far more pressure than the bearing is capable of withstanding, and so immediate failure occurs.

The purpose of the spacer is to keep the bearings from side loading when the axle nut is tightened. It keeps the inner races from moving together as well, and if the outer races are properly aligned, the balls will be in the center.

The length of the inner spacer should be about 0.010 in. greater than the distance measured across the bottom of the bearing bores. If these dimensions are correct, wheel bearings will give many troublefree miles. This is not a common problem, but if wheel bearings fail this is the first area that should be checked out.

Wheel spacing

Wheels should be in alignment with the centerline of the frame. Have you ever followed another motorcycle noticing that it sort of grabs to one side?

The end of the 1987 racing season saw the Dunlop K591 Elite as the tire to win on in Production class racing.

This may be due to a rear wheel that has been adjusted to one side by the chain adjusters, or possibly because of improper wheel spacing.

Another benefit of having the frame placed on an aligning jig is that a good frame-straightening facility can also determine whether the rear wheel is properly spaced. I have found that most motorcycle front ends are symmetrical and the front wheel needs only to be centered between the fork tubes—not the sliders but the fork tubes. They are precision ground and therefore offer a better point of reference.

Tires

If you can't put it to the ground then all the engine and chassis development in the world will do no good and that is where tire companies come in. I have made or modified almost every part on a motorcycle but have never attempted to make my own tires—and with good reason. It's a job much easier left up to those tire company engineers and chemists who do an ongoing job of helping us riders keep that fine line between right side up and road-rash!

Motorcycle tires take a lot of abuse and neglect. How would you like to be somebody's motorcycle tire? I recall reading a statement by a leading tire manufacturer that attended a large motorcycle rally recently and in checking a large number of tires found most to be underinflated. I find this a little disconcerting but not surprising. I doubt that most street riders pay enough attention to their tires. On the other hand, racers are always checking their tires.

Racers have the benefit of trackside service by tire manufacturers on the national level. We have all seen those colorful vans and uniformed personnel at places like Daytona, Laguna Seca and Sears Point. Now we

The Radial slick by Dunlop. With the popularity of radial tires it was only a matter of time until tire makers would develop the concept for motorcycles. The 1987 season saw good success with racers using Radial tires. Radial tires have been OEM on some models of sportbikes since 1986. Looking at the wear pattern of this Dunlop radial shows that the tire came up to the right temperature and the rider was working the tire right to the edge.

Dunlop Tires' concession at Monterey's Laguna Seca Raceway, 1987.

even see them at the club-level events. That is a good sign as it tells me that club racing is becoming important to them. Club racers should get to know their local race-tire distributor because the benefits go both ways.

The distributor needs feedback from the racer for its own development programs.

Since John Boyd Dunlop invented the pneumatic tire in 1888, the basic principle has remained the same

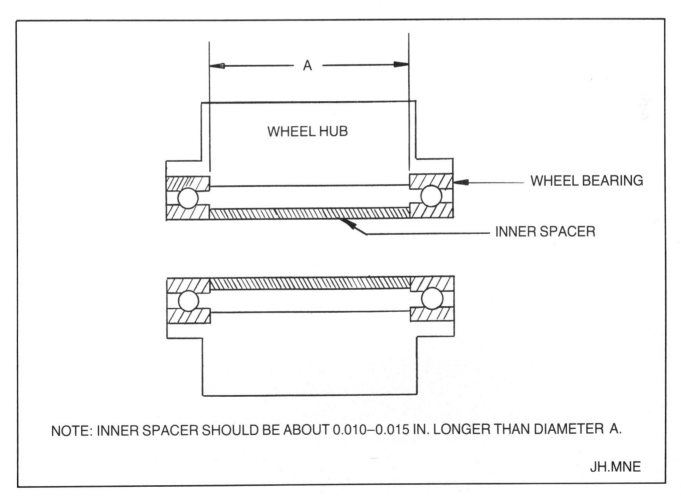

NOTE: INNER SPACER SHOULD BE ABOUT 0.010–0.015 IN. LONGER THAN DIAMETER A.

JH.MNE

but the chemical and structural engineering developments have become quite sophisticated. Now there is all this talk about cross-belted, bias-belted, radial-ply and so on. Tires have a higher aspect ratio, meaning wider tread and lower profile. The radial tire, the choice for the performance automobile, is becoming the word for motorcycles as well. They are not totally perfected yet, but it's only a matter of time before radial-ply tires will be standard equipment. Tire manufacturers are in the business of supplying the consumer with the state-of-the-art product, and it is the responsibility of the consumer to apply the proper principles to that product for the best results.

When selecting street tires we know that these tires are going to be on the motorcycle for a few thousand miles, so we want to make the best choice that is available at the time. Some tire manufacturers, such as Dunlop and Michelin, offer compound options on their sport tires. For ultimate traction the choice, of course, would be the softer compound. If on the other hand mileage is a concern then the harder compound is the choice. Regardless of compound choice for street, you can be assured that your choice of current tires will be the best available at the time. As for maintenance of street tires, just keep them properly balanced and inflated.

At the racing level a good rider may make several tire changes between practice sessions in order to select the right tire and compound for the race. I have seen situations where the tires available on a particu-

The computerized spin-balancing machine used in some motorcycle service facilities.

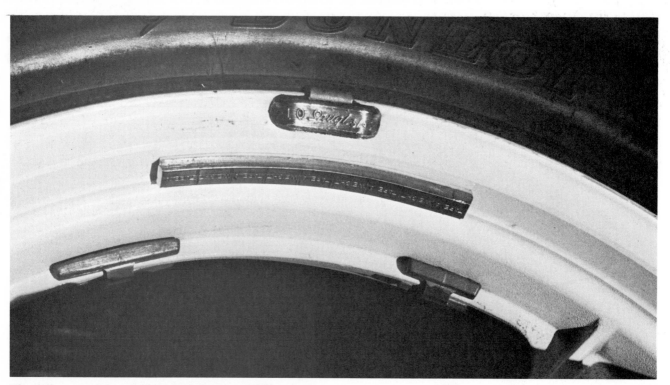

The different weights used in tire balancing. OEM snap-on weights are shown on both the center and outside of the rim. The sticky-back weight rides in a midpoint on the rim.

40

lar race day worked better than the tires available at the next event and vice-versa. Good tire companies are in a constant state of development and minor setbacks should be expected. A good rider will keep an open mind about this.

Tire mounting

Once selected, mounting a motorcycle tire seems like such a simple task. If you choose to do your own mounting, some tools will be necessary such as tire irons, a good-sized rubber or plastic hammer, and rim protectors for the street rider. We don't want to show up for the Sunday street ride with scuffed rims!

A source for compressed air is nice too, as well as a valve stem removal tool, tire pressure gauge and a tire balancing stand. My favorite tire-changing tool is John, who mounts and balances tires at Accessories Unlimited in Newhall, California, with the latest mounting and spin-balancing equipment available. Trackside, your racing-tire man will mount and balance for you—it's all included in the price of the tire.

Before I mount a tire or have it mounted, I like to check the wheel for the heavy side. It is not always at the valve stem. I place the bare wheel on my truing stand and let it seek its low or heavy side. I then make a mark with a grease pen. Tire manufacturers usually mark their tires some way on the light side. When mounting the tire, align this mark with the mark on the rim. Hopefully this will require fewer balance weights to be applied to the rim for balancing in the end.

Balance weights come in several forms. OEM weights snap on to the outside of the rim or to a cast

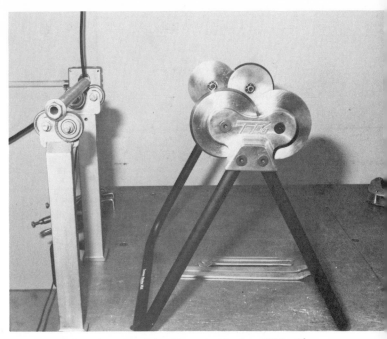

Nice tire balancing stand by Toomey Racing USA. The stand on the left is my homemade unit using the welding table for a base. It makes it a little hard to carry around!

New Dunlop 591 being balanced prior to the 600 Supersport final at Sears Point International Raceway. Even with the new spin-balancing equipment available, the old balance stand still works very well.

Modern tire changing system.

Dunlop's Mark Matzinger has just mounted a new Dunlop Radial for Bubba Shobert and is now checking the inflation pressure.

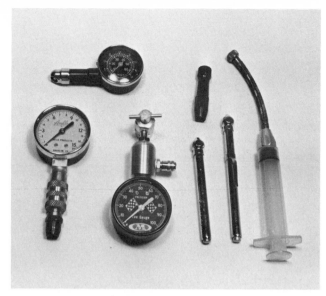

A tire gauge is a necessity to a motorcyclist, particularly the racer. Buy a good one. When at the track check it against the one used by the tire man. The syringe is used to put air in forks and can be checked by the small gauge in the photo. This gauge is made for measuring tire pressures on ATV tires which require very low air pressures.

bead in the center of the wheel. Then there are the sticky-back weights. I prefer the snap-to-the-center bead system. It is simple and is used by most of the factories. Centrifugal force helps keep them in place.

Street riders using sticky-back weights should keep this in mind: the foam rubber between the weight and adhesive can rot in time and the weight will fall off, so inspect the weights once in a while to see that

they are adhering well. In a racing situation, the stick-on type weights are not a problem because tires will be changed more frequently.

Tire pressure

The most important thing on a racing tire is to get the tire to "come in." This means that under proper inflation and use, the tire temperature will increase, the pressure will rise and allow the compound to become

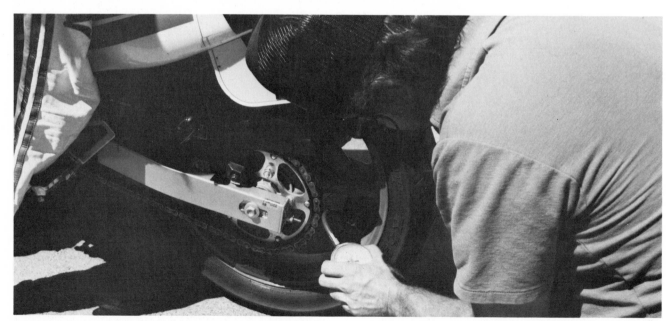

Air pressure is checked on tires prior to laps on the track. Pressure is checked again after laps to document pressure rise. At this time the tire temperature will be checked with a pyrometer. With proper inflation the tires will rise in pressure and temperature to get that optimum adhesion on the track surface.

A piece of 4x6x12 in. wood cut on a diagonal makes a handy tool for blocking the front and rear tire. This makes the job of removing and installing wheels easy.

A short piece of an old rear axle cut to the proper length will hold the rear caliper hanger and spacer in place while the axle is installed from the other side.

sticky, creating that ultimate effect called great traction.

The tire pressure rise should be about ten percent greater than cold; say 4–8 psi, with a cold starting pressure of 32 psi for fronts and about 4–6 psi rise at 36 psi for the rear tire. Check with particular tire manufactur-

ers' specifications. The working temperature for a racing tire should be somewhere in the area of 175–250 degrees Fahrenheit. Depending on the ambient temperature and the track temperature, you can tune your tires by increasing or decreasing the static or cold pressure by a pound or two, remembering that underinflation will cause the tire to run hotter by allowing the

Being overly aggressive on the first lap of practice, or the race, with cold tires can be costly. This Honda Hurricane 600 rider at Willow Springs Raceway ended his day with a slide for life and an incredible repair bill.

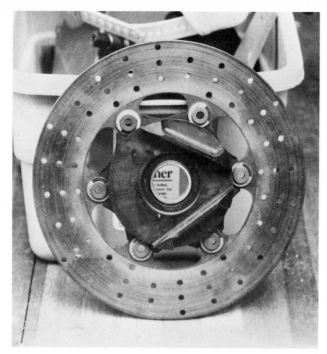

When a quick tire change is necessary, one might wonder how those factory teams do it so rapidly. Here's the secret. The rear brake and disc assembly, with its triangular center section, remains attached to the swing arm when the axle is removed. . .

casings to flex more. Overinflation has the opposite effect, keeping the tire casing more rigid, thus building less heat.

When the ambient temperature rises above 90 degrees Fahrenheit it's a good idea to use nitrogen to inflate your tires if you are faced with overheating or the dreaded "greasy" tire condition, but your pressure rise from cold to hot will be less. This is an alternative to purchasing a harder-compound tire.

One final comment. Be aware of the early morning and late afternoon track surface temperatures. The

. . . and then the rear wheel with a triangle-shaped driver simply slides into the mated part on the disc assembly. This makes for a much quicker rear wheel change.

early morning cool condition may require a little more track time to get the tires up to temperature or less pressure should be used. Remember to check inflation as the ambient and track temperature rises or falls during the day. The competition between tire manufacturers is intense, to say the least. Things can change daily. The choice of tires and compounds by a professional motorcycle racer on any given race day can make the difference between winning and just competing.

Essential tire-mounting and testing tools include the following:

Tire pressure gauge

Pyrometer—if the trackside tire man doesn't have one, which they usually do

Swing arm stand

Front end stand

Frame stand. Not good for full-fairing motorcycles and only allows the removal of one wheel at a time

Tire truing stand

Nitrogen bottle with regulator for tires and shocks and a compressed air bottle

Shortened piece of axle to hold brake hanger in place

Wedges cut from a $4 \times 6 \times 12$ in. block of wood for holding up the front or rear wheel while installing the axle

A serious word of caution to motorcyclists who ride on the street. Racing slicks on your street machine may look impressive at the local gathering place, but they are illegal and very unsafe for use on public roads. Slicks are not designed to work on surfaces that collect oil, water and debris found on public roads.

Brakes

Brakes supplied on most production motorcycles rival those found on racers and in fact, many racers do not bother with aftermarket updates. Take the Suzuki GSXR750. About all that you need to do for production racing is change the pad compound, fit braided steel lines and use premium DOT 3 brake fluid.

DOT 4 or silicone brake fluid is not popular anymore. About all it really did was not ruin the paint on a motorcycle. DOT 4 is a much denser fluid and therefore harder to bleed, and it costs more.

If you own a GSXR750 and you feel you need more brakes, then simply purchase a set of GSXR1000 discs and calipers; I think you will now have plenty of brakes. Remember, however, this sort of modification is not legal under production racing rules, only for Superbike and Superstreet. Oh yes, it is legal for street use but may void your warranty!

Calipers

If it is necessary to update brakes for some reason or another, there are aftermarket products available. Brembo calipers are excellent, along with Lockheed and Spondon. These items can be purchased separately or in kit form including discs, master cylinders and mounting hardware for most popular motorcycles.

If there is not a mounting kit available for your motorcycle, you will have to have one custom-made by someone qualified such as a machinist or fabricator. Be prepared for the extra expense.

Brake disc material

One material used in brake discs today is a material from yesterday, cast iron or meonite. I have seen other materials for discs come and go, such as stainless steel, plasma-sprayed aluminum—even carbon fiber—but good old cast iron seems to be one of those metals just suited for the job.

Avoid drilled cast-iron discs with holes larger than about 0.156 in. Lightening holes any larger than this may cause cracking under intense use and will reduce braking efficiency. Three or four shallow slots per side may be even better. This idea is used successfully in car racing along with cast-in-center venting. This concept is also used by Yamaha on the FJ1100 and FJ1200 with good success. Its only drawback is more weight.

The factory racing machines use a steel that is working well. I do not know what its makeup is—possibly a low-carbon stainless steel—but it seems to be the same material that is used on other production motorcycles, and the material seems to hold up well. It seems to be corrosion resistant and has a low appeal to the presence of a magnet.

Brake lines

Braided steel brake lines are hands down the most efficient lines other than steel tubing. Motorcycles require flexibility and the braided lines afford the necessary flex rather well. Dash 3 braided line has a pressure rating of around 2,000 psi. Even with the master cylinder ratios used, I do not believe it would be possible to burst a line by hand.

Before installing braided steel lines, keep something in mind, particularly street riders. The OEM lines give a little softness to the feel of your brake lever, a softness due to the brake lines expanding until they reach their pressure capabilities. For street riding, I think this is a good idea, especially if you are a new rider. Think about this for a minute: riding on the

This nicely done Ducati 750 Sport has the classic front wheel and disc brake components that were part of the show-stopping character of this motorcycle. The wheel is standard laced with Lockheed twin-piston calipers. Originally the motorcycle came with cast-iron discs—these are very rare Hunt plasma-sprayed aluminum discs. The brake

lines here have been replaced by braided steel aircraft quality parts. In its day, it was state of the art and still rivals the brake systems available on some motorcycles. The motorcycle is not heavily modified but subtly changed to make it stand out.

This Triumph has what I call a set of economy brakes. The motorcycle junkyards are full of Honda calipers and discs just waiting for someone to come along and do what the owner of this Triumph did. These were the first disc brakes on a motorcycle that I remember. I had almost the same setup on my Triumph, and did many installations just like this. This is a 1971–72 Triumph Bonneville in a Trackmaster frame.

street can be full of surprises, and hazards can cause a rider to, as they say, grab a handful of brake. With OEM brake lines, this soft feeling at the beginning gives a more progressive pressure build-up and may just save the front wheel from locking and going away.

I have been using braided steel lines for many years and have gotten used to the sudden response, but have gone to a combination that I like better. I use the OEM line from the master cylinder to the junction block, and braided steel lines from there to the calipers. I also use braided steel on the rear.

Braided steel lines are available in two forms: already assembled or you can make up your own; this is a personal choice. The benefits of making up your own lines are that they are repairable, but the cost of reusable fittings is considerably more. As for racing applications, you will need all the brakes you can get as soon as you can get them.

Brake system bleeding

Bleeding the brake system can go like a dream sometimes, and then other times it's a nightmare. I have tried every product that has anything to do with bleeding brakes. At the 1987 Daytona races, Jeff Stern, Team Jeff's rider whom I was working with, decided to use a set of new Lockheed four-piston calipers on his GSXR750. We spent most of the week trying to get

those brakes bled and to perform at least as well as the stock brake calipers. We also experienced the worst pad taper that the Ferodo rep had ever seen. Near the end of the week we gave up on the Lockheeds and went back to the stock Suzuki calipers and rotors. Later we found out that there was a production flaw in the particular Lockheed calipers we had used.

Consequently, I set out to come up with a simple, effective way to bleed brakes. Back in my California shop I decided to develop the ultimate brake-bleeding system for the motorcyclist. I spent days making a one-way valve of stainless steel with just the right amount of spring pressure on the ball check. It worked great, but I couldn't figure out how to manufacture this system for a reasonable price.

Then I realized that something else was making the bleeding process easier. I had noticed that I was getting air in the vent line from the bleed screw, so I wrapped the bleed screw with about two turns of Teflon tape. That tape wouldn't allow air to pass around the threads of the bleed screw back into the system. A few days later, I was showing an old friend my idea. He thought it was great but suggested that instead of the one-way valve I should just run the drain hose into a gallon jug of water and that would accomplish the same thing. It seems that a hydraulic system needs just a little vacuum in the system to keep the fluid traveling toward the bleed area, and the water in the gallon jug would supply that vacuum.

Give it a try, but don't forget to wrap the bleed screw with Teflon tape. Also, don't let the master cylinder fluid level get too low during the bleeding process. Using this method of brake bleeding, it is not necessary to close the bleed screw until there is no more air in the line. If a dual caliper system is being bled, rotate from one side to the other until there is no more air in the system. Don't worry about how much brake fluid is used. Brake fluid is cheap when compared to the possible cost of having spongy brakes.

Brake pads

Choosing brake pads is fairly simple. They come in various compounds from hard to soft. The softer the compound the better the stopping power and the shorter the service life. The pads that come stock on some motorcycles today are highly metallic and are harder on discs, but they work well and the service life is quite good. High-performance brake pads are produced from asbestos with some metallic content, depending on the particular compound. Remember, the higher the performance the shorter the service; this is something to consider when racing. The distance of

Lockheed four-piston caliper installation on a Suzuki. Four-piston calipers and 320 mm discs add up to plenty of brake!

A John Player Norton with a laced wheel, Lockheed caliper and disc. The system was state of the art in its time. Chris

Scott competes with the motorcycle at vintage race events around the country. This photo was shot at Daytona, 1987.

47

Twin-piston Lockheed calipers, Brembo discs on a Marvic wheel. The motorcycle is a Yamaha YZR250. A good system for a lighter weight motorcycle in the 250 to 300 lb. range.

the race may be such that soft compound brake pads will not go the distance, such as the 200 miles of Daytona. Hard compounds *will* go the distance.

Servicing brake pads is also important. When installing a new set of pads, check the back surface for flatness. If necessary, lap them with emery cloth on a flat surface. This will start the pads out with an even wear pattern.

When new pads are installed, be sure that the pad material does not overlap the outside diameter of the disc. If this is the case, the pad will trap gases that develop during hard braking, which will in turn cause more heat retention made worse by further incessant drag. Heat is the main enemy of performance brake systems.

Installing new pads will push the pistons back into the caliper and the fluid will be forced back into the reservoir. If the fluid level is too high, it can cause the new pads to drag or even lock up the brakes. Check for clearance between discs and new pads when the pads are pushed back all the way. Pads will drag when hot—if hot enough.

Check for pad taper as this will tell whether the caliper is spreading. A small amount of pad taper is acceptable, but if the taper is excessive, it could mean improper torque on the caliper bolts or poor caliper design and quality.

Caliper mounting

I have mounted my share of rotors and calipers, and in doing so have established a procedure that works well for me. I use only the front forks and triple clamps, along with the wheel—a mounted tire is optional. With the front end loose I can mount the forks in a vise.

The wheel spacing must be correct. If necessary, this is done by changing the length of axle spacers or machining new ones.

Once the wheel is spaced and the axle and triple clamp bolts are torqued, I will determine the spacing of the caliper to the rotor. I like to use between 0.062 and 0.093 in. This will more than take care of rotor expansion.

The early twin-piston Brembo caliper. The wheel, forks and discs came as a unit manufactured so that the calipers mounted directly to the fork legs. Nice clean design. I don't think there has ever been a bad Brembo brake system. They look good and work good.

Performance Machine discs and calipers on Dave Emde's Formula USA Yamaha FZ750. The wheels are sold by Performance Machine as well. Good system. Calipers are NC-machined from billet stock aluminum.

A piece of 0.062 or 0.093 in. aluminum welding rod is bent by hand around the outside diameter of the brake rotor and held in place at each end of the welding rod by duct tape. This will space the caliper properly away from the rotor. The aluminum welding rod is soft and easily formed by hand. With a tool made by welding an air hose fitting to a caliper bleed screw, an air line can be attached to the caliper using compressed air to hold the caliper securely to the rotor, giving free hands to take measurements while fabricating caliper mounting plates.

Using a piece of cardboard, I cut out a template that will give me the general size of the aluminum plate I will need. This particular application will require a piece of half-inch plate. The alloy I use is 6061-T6. One hole is drilled and taped in the roughed out plate. The plate can be bolted to one of the fork leg bosses, then the rest of the holes can be marked with a transfer punch. The other holes are drilled and taped. A duplicate caliper hanger is made for the other side.

This installation of twin-piston Brembo calipers was on a 1987 Honda 250 road racer. The stock calipers were Nissin, which the owner considered to be too much brake.

Before final assembly, the caliper mounting bolts are drilled for safety wire.

Rear wheel of Emde's Formula USA bike. Wheels and brakes by Performance Machine.

Customer RZV500 Yamaha. Installation of small twin-piston Brembo caliper with full-floating hanger. The idea of a full-floating rear brake system is to create a parallelogram between all pivot points in hopes of eliminating rear brake chatter under hard braking situations. I question this on the basis that with today's massive front brakes, the rear brake becomes almost ineffective.

Nice installation by Ron Wood on his prototype 500 cc Rotax road racer. Brembo calipers and discs on Yamaha forks and wheel. The 1987 prototype will be updated in 1988 with a 600 cc motor and other refinements like monoshock rear suspension and new bodywork.

Honda the Innovator. Nissin calipers on rotors that mount in a unique way to the disc centers. The wheel is a six-spoke HRC product. Works forks by Showa, a Honda-owned com-pany. Undoubtedly the best brake system in motorcycle road racing. What calipers is Suzuki coming standard with in 1988?

The front end on Jeff Stern's Suzuki GSXR750 superbike. The rotors and caliper are from a GSXR1100 and mounted on a Dymag wheel. Braided steel lines and Ferodo pads complete what is basically a stock system.

Yamaha FZR brakes. The stock system works very well—and that's an understatement. For a standard, off-the-showroom-floor brake, the system is incredible. Add some braided steel lines and Ferodo pads and the system is even better.

Brembo calipers and rotors. Forcella Italia (Ceriani) forks.
All Italian, of course: it's a Ducati F1. Like I said before,
Brembo doesn't make a bad brake system. Looks good,
works good!

Marzocchi forks, Brembo calipers, discs by Erik Buell and a
Marvic wheel. Floating discs allow for differences in expansion due to heat build-up between the disc and the disc car-
rier.

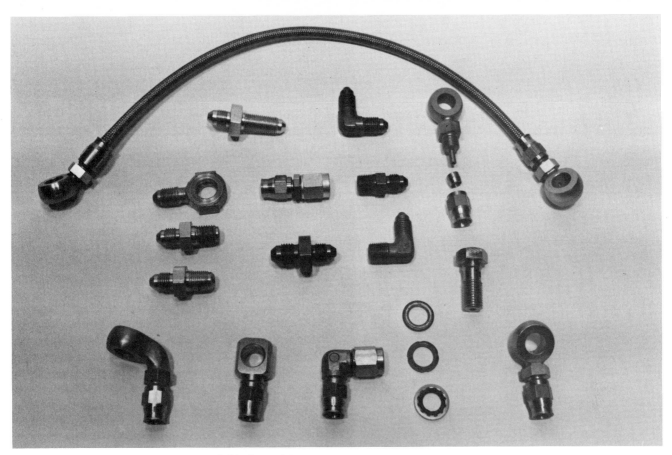

An example of some of the fittings available for making up braided steel brake lines.

Ferodo brake pads have been the racers' choice for many years. Several compounds are available. EBC pads are the competition. Brake pads and compounds are an item that the user will have to decide on through the use of the product. Softer compounds for sprint racing, harder compounds for longer or endurance events.

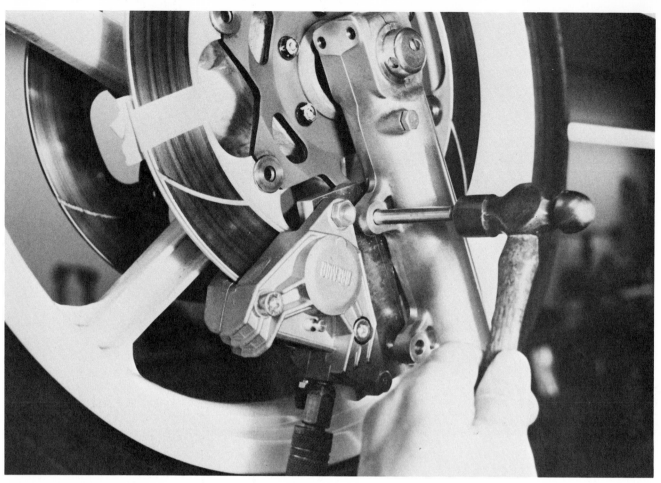

A piece of 0.065 in. welding rod taped to the diameter of the rotor will establish the rotor-to-caliper clearance. With a special fitting, compressed air can be used to hold the caliper to the disc. With the aid of a cardboard pattern, the posi-tioning of the caliper to the fork mounting boss can be established. A hammer and transfer punch is used to mark the center of the mounting plate hole.

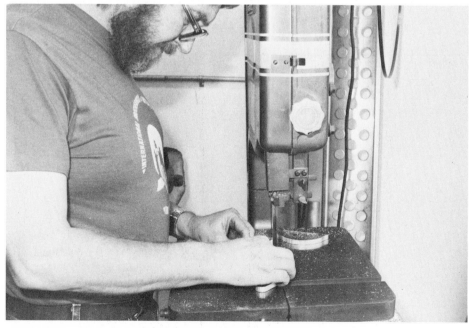

When all the mounting holes have been marked, the caliper bracket is cut to size on a band saw, leaving the line for final finishing on a disc and belt sander.

Using the milling machine as a drill press, the hole centers
are picked up and drilled for tap size.

Again using the milling machine and the chuck, run the tap
in a few threads. The tap is released from the chuck and the
tapping is finished by hand. When drilling and tapping in
aluminum, always use a cutting lubricant. A blend of half
kerosene and half engine oil is good.

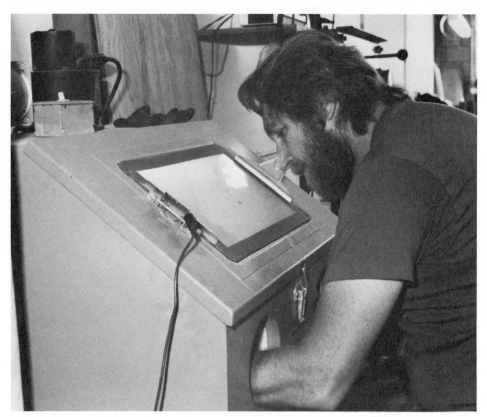

The parts are glass-bead blasted. Bead blasting cleans the part and gives it a nice finished look.

The completed caliper hangers are ready for final assembly. These hangers were required to be offset in order to align the caliper with the disc. The offset was done on a rotary table, leaving a nice round boss on the fork side of the hanger.

Chapter 5

Suspension

The front forks and rear shock, those mysterious devices that keep the wheels of motorcycles firmly in contact with the tarmac, are not really as mysterious as we may be led to believe. Forks and shocks are really very simple. With the help of springs, restricted oil and some air or nitrogen assist, we have suspension units. These units support the weight of the motorcycle and rider over the various little lumps and bumps that we ride on. All things being correct, we have a comfortable, tractable riding situation . . . well, maybe!

Several years ago I had the pleasure of working with my friend Bruce Burness, whose experience with suspension goes back to the days of S&W Products. Burness, later employed by Ohlins shock company in Sweden, worked and traveled with world champion motocrosser Roger DeCoster for many years. One of his last tasks before leaving the company, was developing spring and damping rates for the street motorcycle market. One set of Ohlins was for a Kawasaki project that I was doing for myself, and the data was useful to Burness.

A problem in setting up shocks for the street is that it is more difficult than motocross or road racing simply because the street rider wants good handling in the canyons, where suspension demands were greater, but also wants supple performance for straight-up freeway riding. A classic example of not wanting to give up one thing to get something else! But demands create changes, and so today's performance motorcycles are equipped with adjustable suspension systems! Keep in mind, however, that these are production systems not necessarily intended for competition use or even for what some riders are capable of on the street. Before considering any modifications it would be good to know some basics about suspension units.

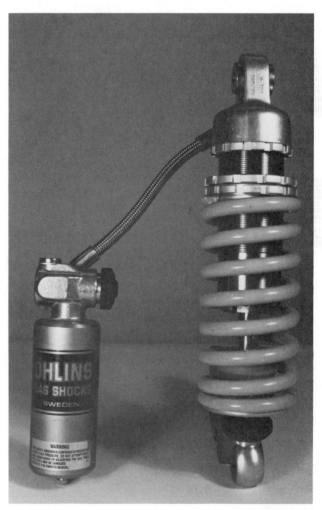

The rear suspension unit by Ohlins of Sweden. This is a very precise, high-quality piece of equipment. The spring pre-load is adjustable along with adjustable compression and rebound damping. This is top-of-the-line equipment. The cost is not that much higher than other available units. Remember, quality costs. Other load shock units are White Powder, Fox & Works Performance. Showa will be available for most motorcycles soon.

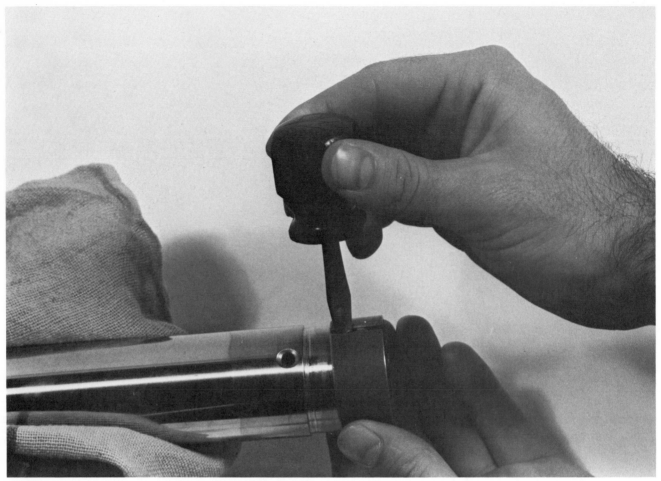

With a screwdriver, the bearing at the bottom of the fork tube is spread just enough to slide it partly off the end of the tube.

Springs

The rate of a spring is the amount of force required to compress a spring a given distance, usually expressed in pounds per inch. A 100 lb. spring will increase by 100 lb. for every inch of compression. This applies to a straight-rate spring.

A *two-rate progressive* spring is one that has the first few coils wound at a different rate. Say the spring callout is sixty/ninety. The advantage of the progressive rate spring is a more supple ride at less demanding conditions, while having the advantage of handling a greater load under more demanding conditions or a progressive rate, as it is referred to.

A true *progressive* spring has its coils progressively wound so that the rate is more linear, or truly progressive.

Rising rate increases the stiffness of suspension by using linkage that will require more force to compress the suspension nearing the top of the suspension range. This allows the shock unit to use a straight-rate spring and lessen damping rates. In reality, the shock does not know it's being used in a rising-rate situation.

Shocks

As the piston travels up and down in the *emulsion-type* shock body, the shaft displaces area or takes up space. Oil does not compress so there is an airspace left in the shock body. As the shaft feeds into the body this air compresses to compensate for the shaft. As the shaft and piston move up and down in the shock body, the oil and air emulsifies or turns to foam.

The disadvantage of this type of shock is that it must be worked to mix the oil and air before it really begins to function. Adversely, if the shock is over-

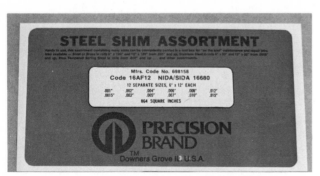

Shim stock can be purchased in an assortment.

Shim stock thickness is determined, and then cut from sheet.

worked, the oil and air become over-emulsified resulting in loss of damping or unpredictable damping. The advantage of this type of shock is that it is simple and inexpensive to manufacture and works all right in less-demanding situations.

In order to eliminate air in a *gas* shock unit, a plastic bag filled with freon gas is incorporated into the shock unit. This does two things: it keeps the air from mixing with the oil and at the same time takes care of the displacement of the shock shaft as the shock is compressed.

The valving in the *De-Carbon* system is precise and responds immediately to changes in the piston position. The piston is much larger and much more

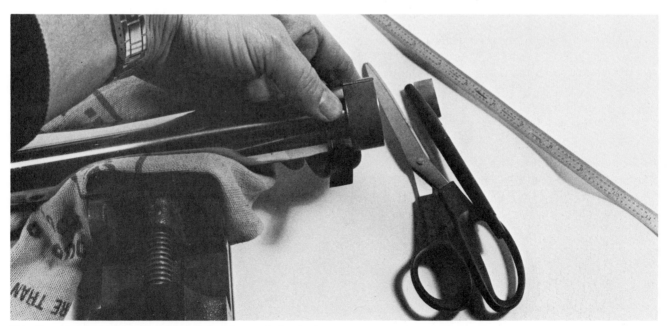

Shim stock strip is placed under fork bearing and checked in the fork slider for fit.

precise. There is a floating piston inside of the shock backed with nitrogen gas. This compensates for the displacement by piston and shaft. This system completely eliminates any air in the shock and the damping becomes consistent. The system has been updated by the addition of a remote reservoir and adjusters for changing the rebound and compression damping. These shock units are expensive, but are by far better than anything in the past.

Front forks

The front forks of a present-day sport motorcycle consist of slider, fork tube, damper assembly and spring; some include air assist. It amazes me how this system has remained almost unchanged since its inception way back when. Telescopic forks are econom-

With bearings in place check the fit of the tube to the slider. The fit should not be too tight, especially on the top bearing.

ical to produce, and they work well. There are some simple modifications that will improve the performance of the current telescopic fork even more.

About 1978, motorcycle manufacturers started to use Teflon-coated bushings at the bottom of the fork tube and at the top of the slider. These bushings greatly decreased the friction between the fork tube and slider in telescopic forks (friction being the resistance between the fork and slider during motion due to the large contact area of the tube and slider in earlier models). In production units, the clearance between the bushing and the slider can be a little excessive, but this clearance can be shimmed. Why do this? Well, if you have say 0.005 in. clearance on the top and bottom bushings, this will allow the slider to move in any direction, at the axle point, say 0.02 in. This is not a good condition for a motorcycle being used in competition—or on the street for that matter.

Start your modifications by disassembling and thoroughly cleaning all parts of the front fork unit. Now measure the diameter of the fork tube bushing while it is still in place on the fork tube. Next, measure the inside diameter of the fork slider. The difference in the dimensions will give you a general idea of the thickness of shim stock you will need. The final fit will be determined by feel.

Shim stock

Shim stock can be purchased in several types in an assorted package or in the longer feeler gauges available from mechanics' tool sources. I use the packaged type because of the variety of sizes, and I can use it for other applications around my machine shop.

Bushings

Before continuing with the shimming, be sure that the top and bottom bushings are in good condition. If the Teflon coating has worn through to metal, replace the bushings. The measurements taken earlier should have a difference of about 0.005 to 0.008 in. We are going to shim a part with a diameter, so we must split the 0.005 to 0.008 in. dimension to get the dimension for each side, which would be 0.0025 to 0.004 in. or the approximate thickness of the shim stock to start with.

Using a screwdriver, split the bushing enough to slide it partly over the end of the fork tube. There is no need to remove the bushing completely unless it's being replaced. Be careful not to distort the bushing. Cut a piece of shim stock about one-half inch wide with scissors. Cut the shim stock to length by wrapping it around the bushing area making sure that it does not overlap itself. Push the bushing back over the shim stock until the bushing snaps into place. Now put the fork tube into the slider with the upper bushing in place to serve as a guide. If the shimming procedure is right, the fork tube should slide up and down in the slider with just a slight amount of resistance. If you are satisfied with the feel then go to the other tube and slider, and repeat the process again. Don't over-shim.

The top or slider bushings should be left as they are. More clearance is needed on top between the slider bushing and fork tube. Under hard braking the fork tubes can distort at the top bushing requiring more clearance to keep the fork tube and slider bushing from binding. This situation can be one cause of the front end chattering during hard braking.

Factory and some aftermarket fork units are built with better and stronger material which allow closer tolerances. The cost of these fork units can be staggering, and are not legal in box stock production classes.

Seals and wipers

Fork seals and wipers are a source of friction as well. The fork seal you must have, but in racing you could throw the wipers away. Fork seal drag becomes greater as it wears because the surface of the lips becomes wider. The ground surface of the fork tube becomes polished and can no longer retain oil to lubricate the fork seal, and the wear process increases. The worst enemy of the fork seal is that tiny rock that smacks the fork tube and creates a micro-knife-edged pit that cuts into the fork seal. We have all experienced the dreaded ring-around-the-fork-tube condition!

There are a few things that you can do to prevent seal failure. Try placing a piece of foam rubber or felt around the fork tube between the seal and wiper. This foam or felt will absorb oil and help lubricate the fork tube above the seal. This requires keeping the wiper in place, but with a small drum sander the clearances of the wiper can be increased. The other thing I do is keep on hand a piece of 400-grit emery cloth or a small Carborundum stone so that when those little seal-eating pockmarks and shiny spots appear on fork tubes, I can quickly do away with them. Rotating the fork tubes about fifteen degrees from time to time will help slow down the shiny-spot condition.

Spring rates

The next tuning on the front forks deals with spring rates. The quality of stock springs today is just fine. Along with the OEM spring comes an air spring, whether the motorcycle is equipped with air assist or not. Inside the fork assembly is an air chamber. When the fork is compressed, the air is compressed, so we have a compression ratio. We can apply one of the laws of physics, Boyle's Law, which simply states that if you cut the volume in half, the pressure will double. So by adding or subtracting oil from the shock you can vary the rate of the air spring, or if you have air assist you can increase or decrease the air pressure, thereby changing the air spring rate.

Keep in mind, however, that subtle changes in air pressure or oil volume can cause radical changes in the air spring rate. Keep air pressure to a minimum: two or three pounds is plenty.

Oil

When using the air spring principle, the actual volume of the assembled fork should be known. The general specifications in shop manuals only call out the amount of oil needed; this is the minimum amount of oil that can be in the fork unit.

To find the volume of the fork unit, start with a clean, assembled unit without the spring. Use automatic transmission fluid (ATF) to fill the fork unit partially full, noting the amount of fluid used. Slowly cy-

Before assembling the forks take a burr knife or small file and remove all the sharp edges around the compression and rebound orifices.

cle the fork tube up and down to fill the valving area of the fork, always leaving the fork tube in the fully compressed position. Continue adding ATF, noting the amount until the oil is up to the bottom threads of the fork tube. Note the total amount of ATF used.

Now the volume of the fork spring—and any shims or spacers if used—must be determined. This is done by constructing a tube with one end closed off that will contain the spring. Fill the tube with ATF, noting the amount of oil used. Empty the oil from the tube, place the spring in the tube and fill again with ATF, recording the amount of oil. The difference between the two recorded amounts of oil is the displacement of the spring. Deduct this amount from the amount of oil in the fork unit and you are left with the total displacement of the fork unit. Remember, this is not the amount of oil to be used in the fork, but the

range to work within to tune the air spring portion of the fork unit.

What all this amounts to is simply overfilling the fork tube, however, remembering that the rate of an air spring rises much faster than that of a wound steel spring.

When tuning the suspension, keep the changes documented and make only small adjustments and in steps. Let the suspension work. Oversprung and excessive damping will not work.

The rear of the motorcycle takes the greatest amount of abuse and needs the most precise amount of tuning. If there are handling problems that are suspension related, work at the rear first. What may seem like a front end problem may be something that is being transmitted to the front from the rear.

The Simons mobile sales and service truck at Laguna Seca Raceway.

Chapter 6

Carburetion, ignition and exhaust systems

Carburetion

In theory carburetors are really simple instruments and not at all difficult to understand, but in practice the more you know the more you begin to realize what you don't know about them. Imagine a single-cylinder engine with no carburetor as we know it today. If you were to get that single-cylinder engine up to a certain rpm and hold, say, a tin can with gas in it near the intake port and punch the right size hole in the bottom of the can, you would have a very simple carburetor . . . and the engine would run (run, yes; run perfectly, no!). Henry Ford knew this a long time ago!

Most motorcycle engines today come equipped with CV (constant velocity) carburetors. I have taken the time to understand CV carburetors and have come to appreciate them; they are great instruments. These carburetors control the velocity of air over the fuel-metering systems dictated by the vacuum of the engine at a given rpm. The slide valve and needle are positioned by vacuum demands from the engine and so the engine never gets more fuel-air mixture than it needs. Today's carburetors are considerably more sophisticated than Henry Ford's and capable of metering the fuel-air mixture over a much wider range.

The Honda and Yamaha factory teams use CV carburetors on their Superbike racers with great success. Contrary to some gossip that CVs are not good top-end carburetors, you only have to check who had the fastest trap speed at Daytona in 1987 to disprove that statement. CV carburetors are also noted for their contribution to harder acceleration out of turns.

To know how a carburetor works, you must understand the different ranges of metering that cover the modern carburetor and where these areas occur. Smooth transition from the starting circuits to the full-open positions are easily arrived at if we understand where the changeover occurs and in which circuit we are operating.

Jetting

In a racing situation the carburetor will be used mainly on the needle and main jet circuits, while the street motorcycle will mostly use pilot and needle circuits.

Understanding the operation areas of the jetting systems is important. Over the years I have seen jetting changes made to carburetors that did nothing because the change was made to the wrong area. The most typical error is changing the main jet of a street motorcycle when the change really needed to be made in the pilot

The smooth-bore carburetor is not new. The Amal GP was designed more than 30 years ago.

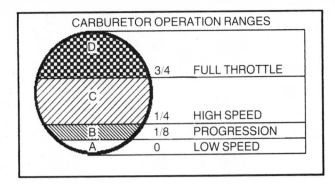

CARBURETOR OPERATION RANGES

D	3/4	FULL THROTTLE
C	1/4	HIGH SPEED
B	1/8	PROGRESSION
A	0	LOW SPEED

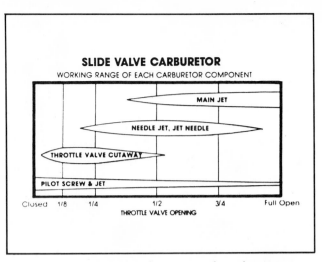

SLIDE VALVE CARBURETOR
WORKING RANGE OF EACH CARBURETOR COMPONENT

MAIN JET

NEEDLE JET, JET NEEDLE

THROTTLE VALVE CUTAWAY

PILOT SCREW & JET

Closed 1/8 1/4 1/2 3/4 Full Open
THROTTLE VALVE OPENING

or needle systems. Learn to know in which area of operation the jetting needs changing.

The accompanying diagram shows the section of a venturi throat according to the operating period regulated by the throttle valve opening. The jetting in each of these areas (A through D) can be changed to suit the fuel-air mixture needed.

• Area A: The low-speed area is controlled by the idle screw and the idle mixture screw, and meters the fuel-air mixture from zero to about 1/8 of the way open through a small hole just ahead of the slide or butterfly valve, depending on carburetor style. On newer constant-velocity carburetors, what would be an air-regulating screw on other types of carburetors is a fuel-

Each metering range in carburetor overlaps the next range. This drawing gives an approximate idea of the overlapping. Knowing this can help in fine-tuning the full range of the carburetor. Yamaha Motor Corporation, USA.

regulating screw; it is most important to know the difference between the two.

For the adjusting procedure, the CV carburetor works exactly the opposite of the other types of carburetors. Turning an air screw in or tightening it will richen the mixture, while doing the same to a fuel

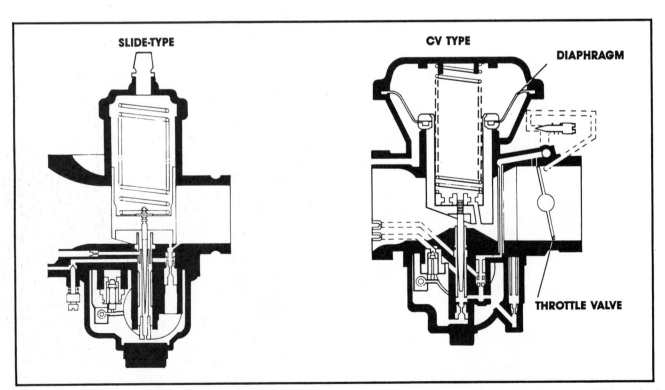

This section drawing of a slide-type and a CV-type shows the different designs of the two carburetors. On the slide-type carburetor the slide is operated by the throttle cable. The butterfly on the CV-type is opened and closed by the throttle cable while the slide is positioned by the vacuum output applied to the diaphragm by the engine. This method supplies the engine with a more constant velocity of air across the metering system. Yamaha Motor Corporation, USA.

screw will lean the mixture. Some older CV carbs have two screws for idle: mixture and volume.

• Area B: In the progression phase, the fuel mixture is steadily replaced by mixture delivery from the pilot outlet hole. The pilot outlet hole is located in front of the idle hole and just under the slide. Mixture in the area is metered by the pilot jet and the slide cutaway.

• Area C: In the high-speed area, the mixture is taken over from the idle and progression period by the needle and needle jet. Any mixture changes will be accomplished by varying the needle position, or changing the needle and needle-jet combination. This area is important and can be critical in a high-performance engine. A lean condition can cause detonation or poor transition into the main or full-throttle range, resulting in poor performance coming off turns.

In street riding, the needle area is the area that is used most often in everyday riding for acceleration. If you understand the carburetor ranges, you will see that not too often do you reach around the twist grip far enough to get on the main jet. Over the years I have seen street riders change main jets, trying to increase performance when they were actually operating in the range of the needle jet and not the main jet.

I have been working with a new Yamaha FZR1000, and when I choose to get it on the main jet I make sure that I have a good hold of that sucker and that there is plenty of space out in front of me! In a racing situation there is an item called the quick throttle which can open the carburetor with about half the rotation of a stock twist grip.

• Area D: Full throttle (WFO), the area of the checkered flag, hopefully the first position. This is the area of the carburetor where the bore and the main jet

Air funnels or velocity stacks on carburetors smooth and direct airflow into the carburetors. Short funnels benefit top-end engine performance while longer funnels work better in the lower rpm ranges. This is another tuning area that becomes very sensitive and is best done on a dyno.

are in play. Choosing the carburetor bore size is very important. Remember, however, that bigger is not always better. Keep in mind that velocity must be maintained over the metering system and that too large a carburetor bore will not help.

New for 1988. The Mikuni 38 mm flat slide racing carburetors for the Suzuki GSXR750. Notice the throttle bell crank is mounted on left side of the unit. This is a nice feature when removing carburetors for jet changing.

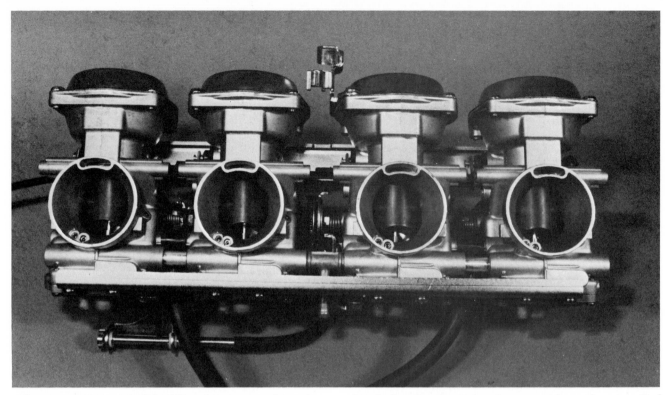

Mikuni 37 mm round slide CV carburetors used on the FZR1000. These carburetors seem to be missing float bowls, but the fact that the carburetors mount in an almost vertical position changes the float bowl configuration.

Synchronize

Be sure that the carburetors are synchronized or that the slides or butterfly throttle valves are adjusted so that each cylinder is pulling the same vacuum at idle. This is done best with an instrument called a mercury manometer. They are readily available from any number of sources. This is the best way to set the idle when more than two carburetors are involved.

Float level

Another very important area that is often overlooked is the float-level adjustment. Why? Because the fuel in the float bowl represents weight. The more

A set of 34 mm Mikuni CV carburetors are a stock item on a Suzuki GSXR1100. They also make a good upgrade for the Suzuki GSXR750. This set went on a stock GSXR750 that was used by Team Jeff for endurance racing events.

weight in the float bowl, the easier it is for the fuel to travel up through the metering system. Inversely, if the fuel level is low it will require more vacuum to pull fuel up through the metering system, thereby causing a lean condition. A difference in 0.5 mm on float adjustment can effect the main jet by one or two sizes. If you find uneven plug readings, the float-level adjustments could be the source of the problem.

Most carburetor manufacturers have catalogs available covering their product line and they usually include a section on carburetor tuning. One such catalog is available from Sudco International Corporation. The catalog has an excellent section on tuning, complete with graphs and charts.

Air filters versus velocity stacks

Running a motorcycle daily on the street without an air filter does not make much sense to me. In a racing situation, however, you seldom see airboxes in classes that do not require them.

In the last four years the airbox units that come stock have improved over past models. I think any good tuner would agree it is better to take intake air from an undisturbed area such as the airboxes of today. I do not think that you can dispute the low- or mid-range performance of the airbox units found on the Honda Interceptors, Yamahas, Kawasakis and GSXR Suzukis.

If you feel that more performance is needed, then try some simple modifications to the intake portion of the stock airbox, along with the installation of an aftermarket filter such as the K&N units. These changes might be just what is needed without giving away what I think is one of the assets of the airbox unit—a reduction in carburetor induction noise. On a long Sunday ride, this induction noise can become pretty

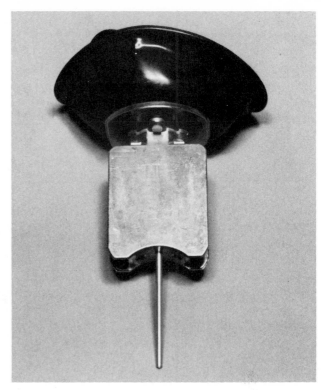

The diaphragm is attached to the slide in a CV carburetor. The slide is raised and lowered in the bore by the vacuum created in the engine. This maintains a constant velocity over the metering system.

annoying. Taking air from a dead airspace and the subsequent absence of induction noise is really a good reason to have an airbox system on a motorcycle engine.

Individual air cleaners are the next choice. They may or may not allow the increase in airflow depending on the application. They will not baffle induction

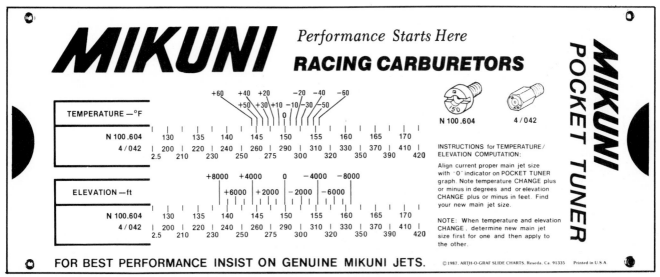

This handy Pocket Tuner from Mikuni American Corporation can help make the proper jet choices depending on changes in temperature and altitude. Other tuning hints and information are on the back. Mikuni American Corporation, USA.

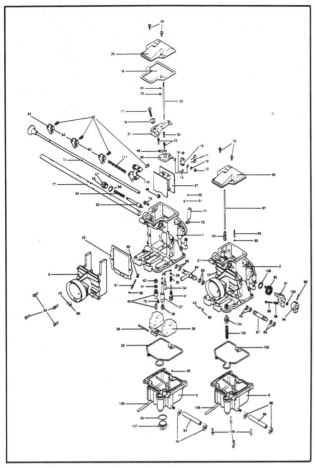

An exploded view of the Mikuni radial slide, smooth-bore racing carburetor. Mikuni American Corporation, USA.

noise and they may be subjected to outside air turbulence. Individual air cleaners will not allow the use in most cases of velocity stacks due to space. Tuned-length velocity stacks can be an important part of high-performance tuning. Remember that any air-cleaner system is better than none!

The only racing classes that require the use of an air filter are the production classes. Most clubs require that stock airboxes remain in place, while the Super-street, Superbike and Open classes run without any air-cleaner systems. Different lengths of velocity stacks will be used.

At the 1987 Daytona motorcycle race there was a new trend set by the Yoshimura Suzuki team. They had placed a sheet plastic shrouding around the carburetors and ducted air from scoops placed in the front of the fairing. Now anyone will agree that an engine would prefer fresh cool air, and it was apparent that this is what the Yoshimura team had set out to do. I also believe that they were creating a dead airspace around the carburetors, not unlike the airbox. The Honda and Yamaha have their carburetors placed almost vertically up under the gas tank out of range of the turbulent air, and fresh air is supplied from air ducts at the side of the fairing. The Suzuki carburetors are placed directly behind the engine and are subjected to more turbulent air. There must be some validity to what Yoshimura was doing because the Suzuki team was right in the top five performers. The concept has caught on at the local club races, and I have even seen the idea on the street.

The butterfly valve in CV carburetors is controlled by the rider at the twist grip and works in unison with the slide.

A line-up of four 33 mm Keihin smooth-bore carburetors transplanted onto a Bimota Suzuki SB4.

Modifying the stock airbox is relatively simple, just a matter of drilling or milling some holes so that the filter element is exposed to more air. A good example is shown in the Dynojet kit for a Yamaha FZR1000. The intake cover on the airbox is removed and a sequence of one-half-inch holes are drilled in the top to allow more air intake.

Servicing an air cleaner is simple. For the common paper filter, a little compressed air from the inside will blow away most of the accumulated dust and give a few more good miles of service. Even so, it's a good idea to replace the filter according to the manufacturer's recommendation found in the service manual. If you are using an aftermarket filter such as a K&N, then the instructions for servicing should be followed by washing in cleaning solvent and re-oiling.

Ignition system

Gone are the days of points, condensers and K-mart coils; we are now in the digital computerized electronic ignition era. I look at these electronic devices as one of the great technological advancements of our time. The electronic units work well, and when they don't work, they don't work at all! But that is seldom. I have a little difficulty with electronic devices because I can't see what's going on, so I simply accept the fact that they work.

Electronic ignitions have been around for some time. In 1976, I purchased a Kreidler 50 cc race motor from Germany. This little engine put out about 16 hp at 17,000 rpm. Not bad for three cubic inches! The electronic ignition system was manufactured by Kro-

ber GmbH. I competed in AFM club events on the West Coast from 1977 through 1979 with the spare ignition never coming out of the box.

The electronic ignition starts with a pickup coil or pulse generator. These units use what is referred to as the Hall Effect, which is based on the development of a voltage across a metal or semiconductor block placed in a magnetic field. Some motorcycles like the Yamaha FZR1000 have one pickup triggered by holes in the end of the crankshaft. The Honda Hurricane has two pickups triggered by a star-like rotor on the end of the crankshaft, and the Suzuki GSXR series bikes have two pickups with a single trigger on the end of the crankshaft. Different as they are, each system sends timed pulses to the spark control unit or, as it is commonly and magically referred to, the blackbox.

The amazing blackbox

The blackbox is a small computer that has the proper advance curve programmed in for the engine. No more mechanical advance systems. Also programmed is a rev-limiter and a sending unit for the electronic tach. The FZR1000 has the control unit for the fuel pump built into the blackbox as well.

The problem with these electronic ignitions comes with changing the advance curve and the rev-limiter as this necessitates replacing the blackbox. With engines in a higher state of tune, the average person is less likely to re-time an engine that may cause some serious damage. There are also clean-air standards that manufacturers must abide by, and a fixed timing curve is one of the ways this is accomplished. If you live in Canada, Australia or New Zealand, where

This Krober electronic ignition system has been around since about 1970.

they still have plenty of fresh clean air, you can bet that blackboxes are different!

If the motorcycle is going to be raced, then it will be necessary to have an ignition system with an opti-

The blackbox used in the Yamaha FZR1000 ignition system.

mum advance curve and rev-limiter option. Start shopping around. Maybe there is an electronic wizard in your area that can re-program that blackbox for your race project.

The sending units on GSXR Suzukis are mounted on a plate. Elongating the mounting holes will enable advancing and retarding of the overall ignition timing. Be careful: a few too many degrees on the advance can cause overheating and detonation resulting in damage to the engine. Other brands have the sending units permanently mounted with adjustment out of the question.

The advance curves are well designed by the manufacturers for production situations, but if the engine is to be modified to a higher state of tune the ignition curve must be modified to suit the needs of the engine. Manufacturers that offer racing kits will include an ignition system designed to meet the needs of a race engine.

Another benefit the electronic ignition offers is the ability to automatically retard the system after a certain rpm has been reached. High-performance engines that run at very high rpm do not need the same advance timing at say 6000 rpm as they would at say 12,000 rpm.

The single sending unit from an FZR1000 is mounted in the right side of the engine case and is triggered by holes drilled in the crankshaft counterweight.

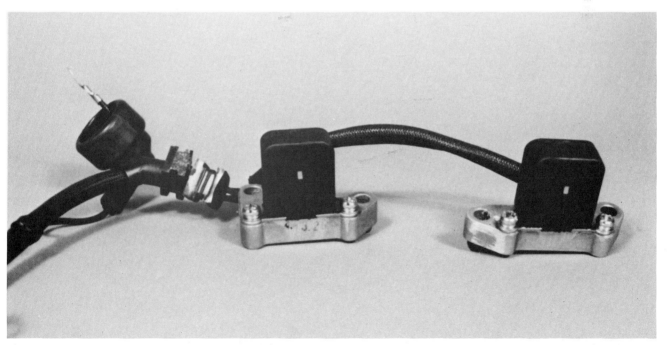

The Honda VF1000 uses two sending units mounted inside the primary cover. These units are dowel-pin located and cannot be adjusted.

The trigger on the starter clutch of the Honda VF1000F.

Exhaust system

I remember George and Esther Kerker building those strange four-into-one pipes in George's garage workshop years ago in Glendale, California. The idea came from the question, if a four-into-one system works on one side of my Corvette engine, why would it not work on my Honda four? George Kerker may not have realized that he was creating an institution as well as a product that is still going strong today. Kerker is no longer with us, but his idea lives on.

Do these aftermarket exhaust systems help performance? Well, they are considerably lighter than stock, they do give the engine a more distinct sound of higher performance and in most cases, they do improve the performance. The amount of performance depends on the state of tune of the engine.

Early Japanese four-cylinder engines did not respond to exhaust system changes like the current engines do because of their lower state of tune. The Kawasaki 900 Ninja, with just the addition of aftermarket mufflers, showed quite a noticeable increase in performance. Add to this carburetor recalibration and cam timing, and the performance was even more impressive. In fact, I do not believe I have ever seen the performance improve as well with just bolt-on equipment as it did on the Kawasaki 900 Ninja. Again the Ninja engine was in a higher state of tune, making it sensitive to changes.

Today, any of the high-performance street motorcycles will definitely respond to the installation of an aftermarket exhaust system, requiring only minor carburetion recalibration.

Exhaust systems are available from Kerker, Supertrapp, Yoshimura and Vance & Hines.

The sending units of the Suzuki GSXR750 are mounted on a plate. The mounting holes have been slightly elongated so the timing can be advanced or retarded depending on the engine's needs. The trigger is pinned to the end of the crankshaft. There are aftermarket triggers available that have the pin slot positioned to change the static ignition timing.

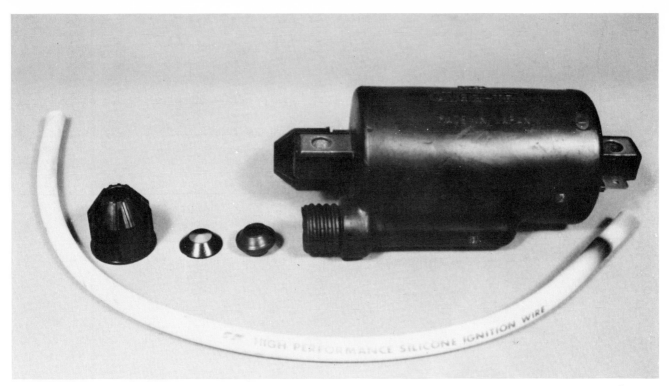

The coils on Japanese performance motorcycles all look about the same and they work very well. There is no need to change them even if the motorcycle is to be raced. The plug wires can be easily replaced because of the very nice collet system used on most OEM coils, but the stock wires work fine along with the plug wire connectors. If the stock system is not faulty, run it!

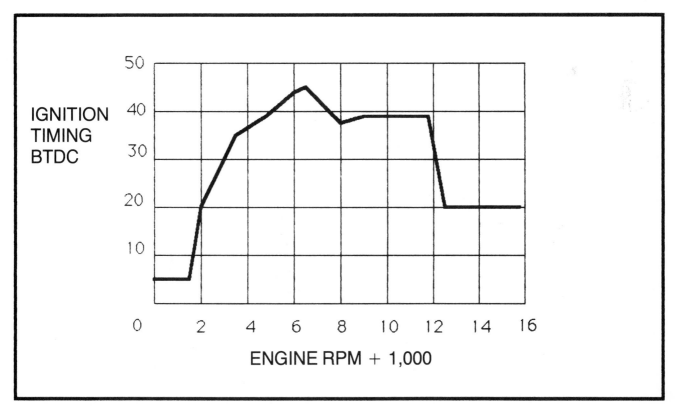

The graph shows the advance curve of the blackbox for a Yamaha FZR750. The curve advances rapidly to forty-five degrees BTDC at 6500 rpm, then tapers off to about thirty-eight degrees at 8000 rpm. The curve remains the same until the rev-limiter cuts in at about 12,500 rpm. One of the real advantages of the programmed blackbox is the fact that the advance curve can advance for maximum engine output in the early rpm and then retard to a better-suited lead time at higher peak rpm.

Yamaha FZR750 and FZR1000. Very clean four-into-one exhaust system by Kerker. All Kerker systems are developed on a dynomometer at the company's facility.

The original Kerker-style exhaust stayed with the motorcycle industry into the 1980s. Here it is shown on a nicely reworked KZ1000J model.

The Supertrapp all-stainless-steel exhaust system on a Bi-mota Suzuki uses the four-into-one approach.

The Supertrapp tailpipe for those not wishing to replace the whole system. These work very well. This tailpipe was available on the 1983 Honda VF750 and 1984 VF1000F.

These stainless-steel spigots, flanges and springs are factory Yamaha components that bolt to the cylinder head of a FZR750 superbike. This is the way the exhaust head pipe is held to the cylinder head. Rather than unbolting the system the springs are removed and the header slides off quickly. The rest of the exhaust system is held together in the same way, except for the bolts holding the muffler and hanger to the frame. The advantage of the springs is simplicity and ease of removing the exhaust system from the motorcycle. You won't find this system used on the street because the exhaust system doesn't need to come off as often as in racing.

Chapter 7

The engine

The engine in today's modern performance motorcycle is really a Grand Prix power unit mass-produced for consumption by the general public. The horsepower output per cubic inch is quite impressive, and the quality of materials and manufacturing tolerances used in making engine components rival that of the aerospace industry.

In this section I will cover the basic concepts of increasing the power output of a typical performance four-stroke four-cylinder engine. There will be an em-

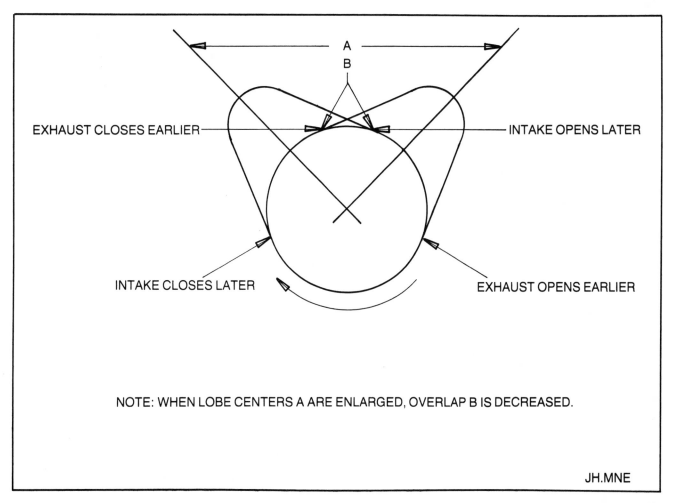

EXHAUST CLOSES EARLIER

INTAKE OPENS LATER

INTAKE CLOSES LATER

EXHAUST OPENS EARLIER

NOTE: WHEN LOBE CENTERS A ARE ENLARGED, OVERLAP B IS DECREASED.

JH.MNE

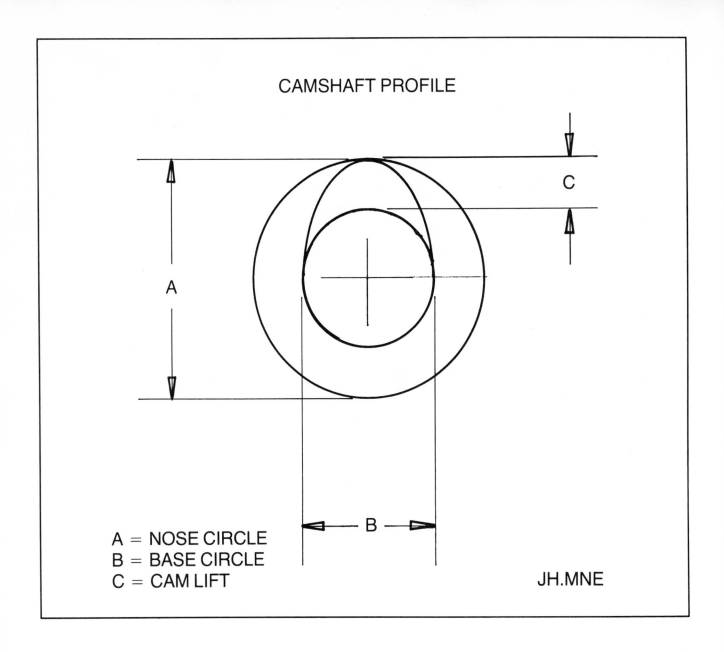

CAMSHAFT PROFILE

A = NOSE CIRCLE
B = BASE CIRCLE
C = CAM LIFT

JH.MNE

phasis on preparing the components and the processes required. Special attention also will be given to preparation for a more reliable machine. Most street riders and particularly beginning racers do not have the kind of money available to factory riders. With good preparation, the engine output can be increased and still maintain good reliability.

State of tune

The horsepower output per cubic inch displacement of a motorcycle engine establishes its state of tune. Increasing the horsepower increases both the state of tune and the engine's sensitivity to changes, particularly jetting and ignition timing. This is evident in the fact that today's higher-horsepower motorcycle engines come with fixed carburetor and ignition settings. Changing these settings can be destructive to a high-performance motorcycle engine because of its higher state of tune.

Modern motorcycle engines are in an incredibly high state of tune when compared to engines of a few years ago. For instance, a 1979 Kawasaki KZ1000 had a displacement of 61 ci, and put out about 68 hp in stock condition, a little over 1 hp per cubic inch. Increasing the state of tune could bring the engine up to 125 hp or over 2 hp per cubic inch.

Today's competition Superbikes at 750 cc produce the same horsepower as past 1000 cc bikes because engines are now in a higher state of tune. How are these higher horsepower figures achieved? One way is through volumetric efficiency.

Volumetric efficiency

Improving the volumetric efficiency is simply getting a larger amount of fuel-air mixture into the combustion chamber, compressing it, igniting the charge and then exhausting it. This sounds pretty simple, and it is, to a point. Beyond that point, however, those tenths of a horsepower come with a considerable investment of time, energy and, of course, money! Those who go after those tenths of a horsepower are the racers you'll see high up in the results of the last competition.

Compression ratio

In my opinion raising the compression ratio of a normally aspirated street-orientated internal combustion engine will do more to increase performance than any other modification. Normally aspirated means the use of carburetors and atmospheric pressure only.

In the last few years, compression ratios for street performance motorcycles have risen from 9:1 to over 11:1. This accounts for a good portion of the increased performance levels that are evident today. With higher compression comes more heat build-up, the reason for liquid cooling. Liquid cooling can also be oil cooling, as is the case with Suzuki's GSXR series motorcycles.

There are two ways to define compression ratios, actual and theoretical. Actual compression ratio accrues while the engine is running. When the engine is running, the valves are opening and closing and all sorts of things are happening. Metal is expanding and clearances are changing and so on. If you think about it, it's almost impossible to measure. Nevertheless, I imagine that somewhere in the world there is an instrument that can measure exact compression ratio, but I am not aware of one. Besides, if you have the proper compression ratio using the theoretical method, it will show up by the simple fact that the engine performs better.

Computing compression ratio

Theoretical compression ratio is easy to measure, and is the method used by good engine builders. It is the ratio between the volume of a cylinder's combustion chamber when the piston is at bottom dead center, versus the volume of a combustion chamber when the piston is at top dead center. This ratio is a very important set of numbers when building a higher-output motorcycle engine.

To compute compression ratio, place the piston at top dead center on the compression stroke when both the intake and exhaust valves are closed. Remove the spark plug, and using a burette or a syringe fill the combustion chamber with automatic transmission fluid to the lowest thread on the spark plug hole. Note the number of cubic centimeters of fluid that has been used. Next measure the volume of the cylinder with the piston at bottom dead center. Divide the larger volume number by the smaller volume number to determine the theoretical compression ratio.

Once this ratio has been established, the ratio can be changed by increasing the size of the piston dome, decreasing the volume of the combustion chamber or using a thinner head gasket when available. Remember, when reducing the combustion chamber volume or increasing the piston dome, keep in mind the relation of the valve to piston clearance. Be aware that every time you change something, it has some effect on some other component in the area.

Camshafts

There are only a handful of people who are knowledgeable enough about camshaft dynamics to design a successful cam profile and then manufacture the product. One of these people is C. R. Axtell of Sun Valley, California. I have spent a few hours, to say the least, in Axtell's facility watching the goings-on and

In order to change the cam timing the cam sprockets must be slotted.

Cam sprockets are slotted on a milling machine using a rotary table. The holes are elongated five to eight degrees to either side of the original holes.

Necessary tools for cam timing include the following: a dial indicator with magnetic base (the small steel plate can be fastened to the cylinder head for the magnetic base to attach to); a top-dead-center pin made from an old spark plug and a cap head screw.

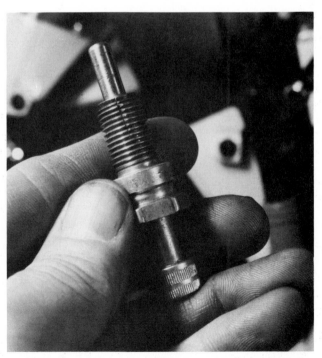

A top-dead-center pin is essential for cam timing. It can be made from an old spark plug and a cap head screw. The end of the screw is slightly rounded so it will not damage the top of the piston.

With the TDC pin and degree wheel in place the crankshaft is rotated in either direction until the piston contacts the TDC pin.

The crankshaft is rotated in the opposite direction against the TDC pin. The numbers on the degree wheel are noted for both directions, 42½ and 32½. The difference is ten. Divide ten by two and we get five which is how far the degree wheel is from TDC. Move the pointer to the right five degrees. Go through the procedure again until the same number comes up either side of TDC. Remove the TDC pin.

learning what I could. Watching a camshaft take shape is an especially interesting process.

These are some of the terms commonly used in the camshaft business:

The *nose circle* is the diameter at the nose or top of the lobe of a cam. The nose diameter also determines the size of the material needed for a billet camshaft blank. Cast-iron camshaft blanks come with an oversize lobe configuration cast in requiring less material removal to finished part.

Base circle is the constant diameter of the cam lobe where no lift occurs. Base circles must maintain a certain dimension in order for the cam follower to remain in its range of adjustability. Rocker arm systems and adjustable tappets have the greatest latitude of adjustment, while the bucket and shim method is somewhat limited. These situations must be taken into consideration in the design of a camshaft profile. The base circle is also the area used when setting valve clearance.

The total amount of lift off the base circle by the cam lobe is called *cam lift*. The nose circle minus the base circle equals the cam lift. This is a theoretical number in cases where rocker arm ratios are used that increase the overall valve lift.

The time, in crankshaft degrees, that a valve is held open by the crankshaft is known as *duration*.

Overlap is the period of time when the intake and exhaust valves are open at the same time at top dead center. Cam timing at this point is critical. If during overlap the valve positions in the combustion chamber are incorrect, the intake valves can collide with the exhaust valves. This condition is critical in older two-valve hemispherical combustion chambers with the installation of higher-performance camshafts. It's not so critical in four- and five-valve pent-roof combustion chambers used in present-day engines, however, because of lesser valve angles and better spacing of the valves.

It is good to think about what actually happens while the engine is in the overlap stage. As the exhaust valve is closing, the intake valve is opening. If this sequence is timed right, the escaping exhaust gases will cause a pressure drop in the cylinder and aid the intake charge. If the exhaust valve closes too soon, gases may be trapped in the cylinder and work against the intake charge, even forcing it back out the intake port. If the exhaust valve is open too long, part of the intake charge may go out the exhaust port. Finding the best

With the dial indicator in place and set against the valve lifter or bucket and the camshaft in the no-lift position, the dial indicator is set at zero.

With the dial indicator set at zero, readings can now be taken from the degree wheel.

Turn the crankshaft in the direction of engine rotation until the cam lifter deflects the dial indicator to 0.04. Degree wheel reading is 18½ degrees.

All readings on the degree wheel are taken at 0.04.

cam timing for a particular engine and situation is what one phase of tuning is all about.

The *lobe center* is the center of the opening and closing of a camshaft. The lobe center system of timing camshafts has been used by successful tuners for years and is the simplest method for timing camshafts. The method will give a lobe center number. Remember, it is only a number!

Camshaft timing

The first step in camshaft timing is to find top dead center of the crankshaft on number one cylinder. I do not recommend using the timing marks on the ignition side of the engine as these marks are relatively accurate but not accurate enough for cam timing.

The best way is the positive piston stop method using a top-dead-center pin. The TDC pin can be made by using a discarded spark plug of the proper thread size. A piece of 5/16 in. rod with one end rounded off will be needed as well. After removing the ceramic portion of the spark plug, the rounded rod is brazed into the plug body so that when it is placed back into the spark plug hole, the piston will stop against the TDC pin at about ten to twenty degrees before TDC. At this point, care must be taken not to use excessive force when bringing the piston against the TDC pin.

The next step is to attach a degree wheel to the crankshaft. Degree wheels are readily available through motorcycle and automotive parts stores. Some adapting may have to be done to attach the de-

gree wheel to the crankshaft. Be creative! Once the degree wheel is in place, a pointer will be needed. A piece of wire with one end filled or ground to a point will do. Attach the pointer somewhere above the degree wheel. Before installing the TDC pin be sure you are on the power or exhaust position of the stroke because if you are on the intake stroke there is a possibility that the intake valve or valves could come in contact with the TDC pin.

With the TDC pin installed rotate the crankshaft forward against the TDC pin—carefully. Set the degree wheel to read TDC at the pointer. Rotate the crankshaft in the opposite direction until the piston contacts the TDC pin. Read the number of degrees from TDC to the pointer and divide by two. Without moving the crankshaft reset the pointer or the degree wheel to the number answered. Remove the TDC pin and rotate the crankshaft until the pointer is at TDC on the degree wheel. The piston is now at top dead center. Go through the procedure again to make sure things are correct.

Before starting the cam timing procedure it is a good idea to have the valve clearance adjustments to the measurements called out by the cam manufacturer, or those called out in the manual for the particular motorcycle engine being worked on. The cam chain should also be in adjustment. Most cam opening and closing numbers are read at 0.04 in. of valve lift. Use 0.04 in. of valve lift when degreeing cams. This will put you past the acceleration and deceleration ramps on the cams and establish an accurate lobe center number.

A dial indicator will be needed to measure the camshaft lift at the top of the valve spring retainer or bucket, depending on the type of system used for a particular engine. As the crankshaft is rotated forward, a reading on the degree wheel is taken at 0.04 in. of valve lift on opening and at 0.04 in. of valve lift before closing. At each of these readings note the number on the degree wheel designated by the pointer. If the pointer falls between the full degree mark, count it as half a degree. These are the opening and closing numbers in crankshaft degrees. Write them down and go through the procedure again to double-check.

Next, take the smaller number of the two and subtract it from the larger number. Add 180 and divide by two to get the lobe center number. (Example: 49 – 25 = 24, add 180 = 204, divide by 2 = 102.) The camshaft just measured has a lobe center of 102.

The lobe center number is just a number to be used to time camshafts in relation to the crankshaft.

Changing the lobe centers of the camshaft requires slotting the camshaft drive gear or sprocket so that the camshaft may be advanced or retarded in rela-tion to the crankshaft. What is the advantage to this procedure? Opening the intake cam sooner does two things. First, it allows the fuel-air intake cycle to start sooner for better cylinder filling, and second, it closes the intake valve sooner, increasing compression. Re-timing the exhaust camshaft will let exhaust gases out sooner or later depending on the demands of the engine.

Remember, the lobe center numbers are only numbers to be used for timing camshafts. Do not forget that changing these numbers also affects the important overlap period. Changing the lobe center numbers can produce some good performance for your motorcycle engine, but finding the right number combinations will be up to the individual through development for there are no set numbers for any given situation.

Cylinder-head preparation

Flow-testing a motorcycle cylinder head is one of the most interesting things that I have done involving a motorcycle engine. After about eighty hours of work on a good friend's flow bench, my Honda 550's cylinder-head final test figures were considerably better than what was supposed to be possible at the time (1977). The best improvement in flow on the cylinder

Rotate engine forward until dial indicator reads 0.04 before the valve closes. The degree wheel reads 53½ degrees.

The *flow bench* measures airflow through the cylinder and is measured in cubic feet per minute. Fixtures are used to open the valves in increments up to the maximum lift of the camshaft. Open port readings are also taken and compared to those with the valves in place to determine the improvement made by reshaping the valve and valve seat area.

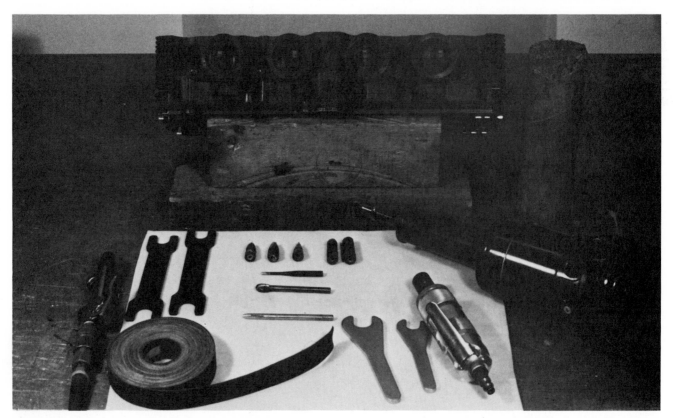

The tools used in porting a cylinder include high-speed die grinders both air operated and electric. Main material removal is done with carbide-tipped cutters. Smoothing is done with cartridge rolls and the final finish with emery cloth wrapped around a steel mandrel. The cardboard tube to the right is a compound used to keep cutters from loading with material from the cylinder head.

This air-powered die grinder turns at 20,000 rpm.

The electric die grinder turns 12,500 rpm and is heavier.

The intake ports are first matched to the carburetor boots. Then it's on to some serious porting and flow testing.

head came in the area of the valves and seats. By changing the profile of the valve and its relation to the valve seat, the flow increased considerably.

The standard angle for a valve and seat is forty-five degrees. Secondary angles on the valve and seats will further increase the flow, but these angles can only be determined by experimenting until the maximum increase in flow is reached. This process takes many hours of work and cost can be high. Today's performance motorcycle engines have four and five valves per cylinder which makes for even more work, plus the fact that valves and ports are considerably smaller, making the work even more difficult, exacting and time consuming, and the cost often staggering.

Today's street rider and club racer in many cases may not be able to afford the cost of a well-prepared and flow-tested cylinder head. If it is affordable, then by all means do it. One suggestion is, be sure the person doing the work has a flow bench and a reputation for doing good work. Be sure also that you are pro-

vided with a flow chart to show the results of the work done.

The current performance motorcycles have cylinder heads that flow enough air to rival the best ported and flow-tested cylinder heads of just a few years ago. The better the cylinder filling, the more the horsepower potential. The cylinder head is still the one area of the engine that if affordable will give the largest increase in performance, if done properly. I recommend, however, that the time and money be spent *only* if serious competition is in order.

The racing valve job

If cost is a consideration, then what is referred to as a racing valve job may be in order. I mentioned earlier that a good increase in flow can be gained in the valve and seat area. The face width of a stock valve is very wide, the seat face being the area of the valve that contacts the seat in the cylinder head. If the seat in the head is enlarged so that contact is higher with the valve face, the size of the port opening at the seat becomes larger allowing more air to pass into the combustion chamber. It's like installing a larger valve without the expense of one.

Narrowing the contact area of the valve to match the seat area is another consideration. This is done with a second cut at a sharper angle below the face of the valve. The underside of the valve can be reshaped for better flow, but with sixteen valves to do I would recommend the installation of good aftermarket stainless-steel racing valves which are already contoured for improved flow.

Valve guides

Valve guides are an item not to be overlooked when preparing a performance cylinder head. A guide that is too tight can cause a valve to stick in the open position, and a valve through the piston is not a pleasant thing to have happen at speed. The impact on the budget will be severe too.

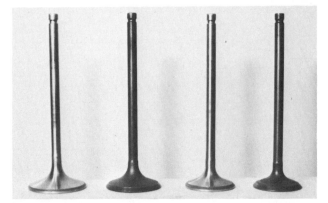

The difference in the shape of an aftermarket racing valve is evident here. They are made of stainless steel. The heads are one millimeter larger and the head profile has been thinned for better flow. Notice too that the seat area is much thinner.

The high-speed stone is the best method for grinding seats. The stones screw on mandrels and are shaped on the stone dresser with a diamond-tipped tool. The pilot guides the stone so the seat is ground concentric with the valve guide. Other tools shown here are lapping compound and a lapping stick.

Worn guides allow the valve to float around on the seat during the closing cycle, causing excessive wear to the seat and valve face. Loose guides will pass more oil. Excessive oil in the combustion chamber is not desirable.

If the guides are bad, replace them just before doing the final touches of a valve job. Leave the old guides in if porting and flow-testing is to be done. Knock the old guides partially out so that the top of the port can be worked on. The old guides will be good enough to support the valve during porting and flow-testing. New guides will be installed for the final touch up of the valve job and assembly. When removing old valve guides heat the cylinder head to about 250 degrees Fahrenheit and use a drift to drive them out.

The same procedure is used for installing new guides except for using some lubricant on the valve guide. Lanolin is good. Some grease or oil will also work.

Once the guide is installed, the guide-to-valve stem clearance is checked. The dimensions will be called out in the specifications section of the workshop manual of the motorcycle engine being worked on. Use a hand reamer to size the guide. A hand reamer has a tapered nose which centers the reamer as it passes through the guide bore. These reamers are available from motorcycle parts departments or a ma-chine tool store. Be sure to specify the correct reamer size for the application.

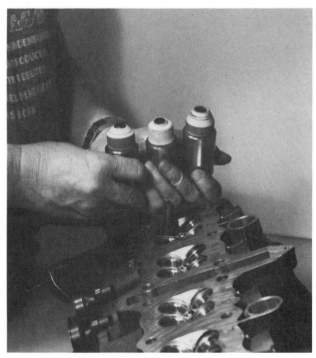

Each stone is dressed to the desired angles.

The angle being cut on a stone. The dresser is easily adjusted to the cutter angle needed.

The final seat preparation must be done with the new guides to ensure that the seats are concentric with the new valve guides. I use Neway cutters for roughing valve seats, but use the stone-type seat cutters for the final seat finishing. Lapping the valves to seats with fine lapping compound is the last step before final assembly of the cylinder head.

An angle being ground on a seat. It is very important to have the cylinder head placed so that the pilot is straight up and down so that the weight of the grinder does not force the stone to one side. The seats must be concentric to the valve guides in order to have good valve seal.

Valve springs

Valve springs are better today than they have ever been. The four- and five-valve cylinders use much smaller springs than the old two-valve heads. It is not uncommon to use a set of stock valve springs in a GSXR750 all season. Jeff Stern's Suzuki logged somewhere in the vicinity of 2,500 race miles in one season of club and professional racing. When I checked the springs at the end of the year they had lost only about two pounds of pressure throughout their range. The engine runs at near 13,000 rpm and is equipped with Yoshimura stage-two camshafts. Not bad service for a stock spring, particularly since the same springs lasted through a second season.

It is a good idea to use aluminum or titanium spring retainers. They are lighter, but should fit into the springs with a slight press fit. This keeps the springs from moving around and lessens the contact between the inner and outer spring. Tighter tolerances also lessen the chance of the valve keepers coming out at high rpm. The lower spring retainers are made of steel and should also fit the springs with a slight press fit.

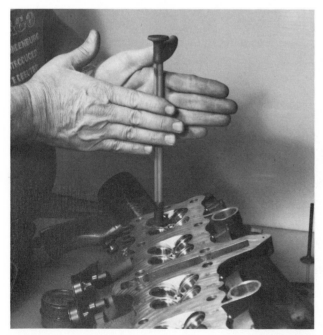

Lapping the valves is done after all the valve seats have been shaped with the seat grinding tools.

The pencil points to the finished valve seat. When all 16 are
done it's time for final assembly of the cylinder head.

These valves have multi angles ground on them. It requires
precision work for the small valves in today's performance
motorcycles. In order to maintain accuracy, I do these small
valves using the lathe and a tool post grinder.

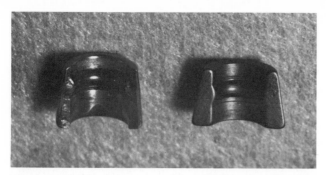

The two valve keepers pictured are of different angles. The keeper to the right is stock GSXR750 Suzuki and has a shallow angle compared to the other keeper. The keeper to the left is more desirable with aluminum or titanium spring retainers. Make sure that keepers are compatible with the spring retainers.

A spring pressure tester is used to determine the installed height of the valve spring assembly. The spring and retainer assembly are placed in the tester and compressed until the seat pressure figure is attained. At this point the height of the spring assembly is measured; this will be the installed height. Some shimming may be necessary. The spring tester can also be used to show the spring pressure at full camshaft lift and to show spring pressure loss.

Installed height is important when setting up the valve springs. The installed height is the length of the springs when installed to provide the recommended seat pressure of the valve on the seat. The seat pressure should be specified by the camshaft manufacturer, and this figure should be maintained. There is no need to have more spring pressure than is necessary! With current technology and progressive cam profiles, valve float is almost unheard of.

Installed height is determined with a spring-pressure-testing instrument with the inner and outer spring assembled into the top and bottom retainers. The spring assembly is compressed to the desired pressure and the height of the spring is measured. The spring assembly is then placed in the cylinder head and shimmed to the desired height. It is a simple operation and must not be overlooked! Always check to see that the top spring retainer does not contact the valve seal at full camshaft lift. If these seals are damaged, oil will pass into the cylinder and can be mistaken for bad ring sealing.

Cylinder-head milling

To increase the compression ratio, cylinder heads will need to be milled. This simply makes the combustion chamber smaller. I mill the head to the almost-finished size before I do anything else. Sometimes it is necessary to cut into the valve seat area of the intake seat. This is the case with Suzuki GSXR750 and GSXR1100 heads. You can then reshape the valve seat properly. This requires lowing the intake valve seat deeper into the head, just enough to get the seat width needed.

Remember that lowing a valve deeper into the chamber also increases the volume of the chamber, but this process must be done to develop a performance cylinder head with the right amount of combustion chamber volume. When the valve job is complete, a final surfacing of the cylinder head is done and the volume of the combustion chamber is checked with a burette to see that you have achieved the final compression ratio that you desire.

This is another area of preparation where coming up with the right numbers is involved. There are no set numbers for compression ratios; good engine builders will develop their own set of numbers as to what works and what does not work. These numbers will in most cases not be given out by a good tuner. But with these suggested procedures you can develop your own set of numbers and keep them to yourself.

Important: When increasing the compression ratio by milling the cylinder head keep in mind that the valve-to-piston relationship is changing as the valves are getting closer to the piston. Use modeling clay to check the clearance. It is necessary to assemble the engine to do this; keep an old head gasket around for this work as well. A good rule of thumb is to have at least 1 mm (0.04 in.) of clearance between the piston and

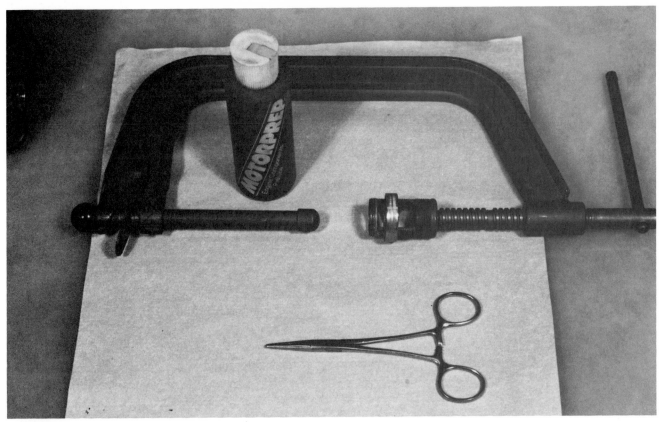

A valve spring compressor, hemostat and assembly lube are
necessary tools when putting the valves and springs into the
cylinder head.

The cylinder head is secured to the mill table. With a large-
diameter cutter, material is machined from the head until
the right combustion chamber volume is reached.

valve face, and between the side of the valve to the valve pocket. The camshafts must be timed properly and valve clearance adjusted when checking valve-to-piston clearance. At the same time the valve-to-valve clearance during overlap can be checked. This clearance should also be about 1 mm (0.04 in.). These processes must be done when building a high-performance engine.

A word of caution: Honda engines with gear driven cam systems cannot have their compression increased by milling the cylinder head. This will disrupt the fit of the gear drive system. Compression can only be increased by installation of higher-compression pistons.

Cylinder boring

Boring a motorcycle cylinder is one of those machine shop operations that I can relate to very well. It is important that cylinder boring is done properly by

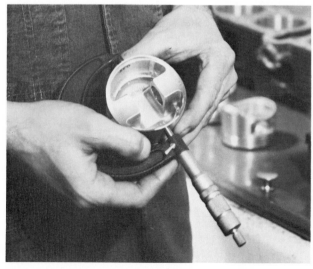

The combustion chamber volume is measured with a burette during the milling procedure. A compression ratio figure should have already been established so that the combustion chamber volume can be machined to that figure.

The piston is measured with a micrometer. To this figure is added the piston-to-cylinder clearance number.

A precision bore gauge is set with an equal precision micrometer to the piston size plus the amount of piston-to-cylinder clearance needed.

someone who is well equipped and knows how to operate that equipment. Most importantly, they must have an understanding and a feel for what they are doing.

My long-time pal Duran Saavedra agreed to let me watch and document this cylinder-boring operation. I made sure the Suzuki GSXR750 cylinder was as clean as possible before I brought it in. There is nothing more unpleasant than having someone bring a part into your shop that looks like it just came out of a bottomless grease pit!

The cylinder is clamped to the underside of a precision-ground table. The boring bar is then positioned over an opening in the table that allows the bar and cutter to pass down through the table to the cylinder. Three pins in the bottom of the bar center the boring machine to the center of the cylinder bore. The boring machine is then locked in place to the table.

Pistons are measured with a micrometer. The piston-to-wall clearance is added to the piston dimension and a precision bore gauge is set at that figure with an equally precise bore gauge micrometer. These measuring instruments are capable of measuring to one ten-thousandth of an inch, or as written, 0.0001 in. The bore gauge is also used to indicate how straight or tapered the cylinder walls may be, a tapered bore being unacceptable. Another micrometer is set and used to place the cutter into the boring head less 0.005 to 0.01 in., as the finished size will be done on a honing machine.

A Sunnen precision honing machine is used for the final operation of the cylinder-boring procedure. The correct size mandrel is installed and a set of 600-grit stones are put in place. A sizing sleeve is run back and forth over the stones to make them parallel and also to produce an arc on the stones that will match the arc of the cylinder wall.

The cylinder bores are passed over the rotating mandrel and material is honed away to the finished size. This is done a little at a time while checking size and parallelism with the bore gauge. The cylinder is reversed front to back on the mandrel to help maintain a straight bore. Proper action across the cutting stones ensures a good cross-hatch pattern necessary for good ring seating and oil retention.

When the bore gauge indicates that the desired bore dimension has been reached, a last check is done with a feeler gauge. This is where the real mechanic comes in—knowing just how much tension is required to pull the feeler gauge between the piston and cylinder wall.

The pistons are now numbered in their respective bores and all parts are given a good cleaning in a solvent tank and dried with compressed air. A little WD-40 or similar moisture-dispersing oil will keep the cylinder walls protected until final assembly. A final

The cylinder is placed and secured onto the boring bar table. The boring bar cutter is set with a micrometer that is part of the system. This procedure is repeated until all four cylinders have been bored to a rough size.

cleaning before assembly with a good dishwashing detergent, a plastic bristle brush and plenty of hot water is a must. I mean clean like a dinner plate!

The lower end

The lower end setup is time consuming and must be done properly; the results will be worth the time and effort. The use of a precision bore gauge will give the important clearance that makes up the oil bearings for the main and rods.

Japanese manufacturers supply bearing inserts in a number of sizes so that you have a range to choose from. The clearances called out in service manuals

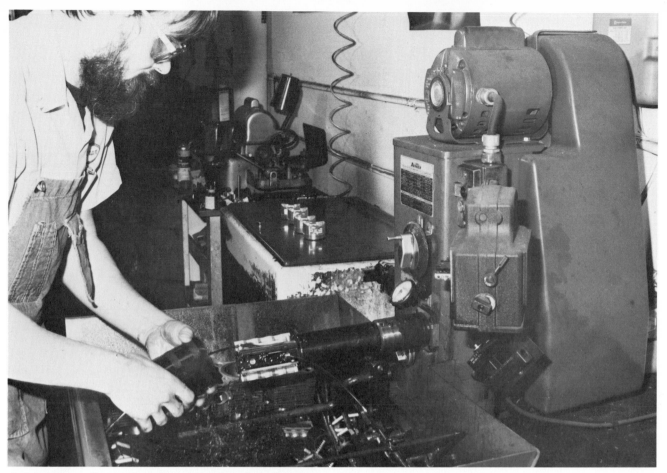

A sizing sleeve dresses the stones to match the arc of the cylinder wall.

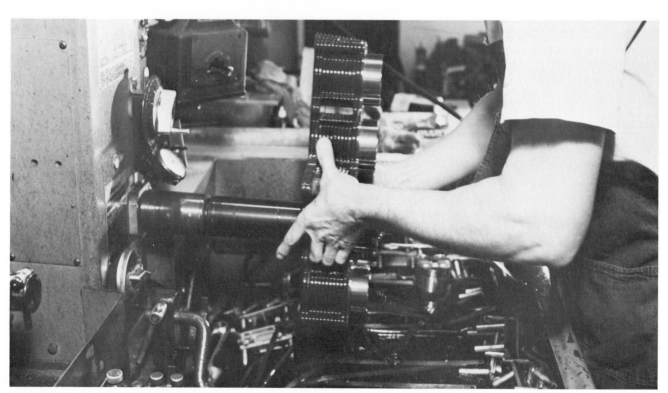

The cylinder is passed over the mandrel to remove material in cylinder. The bore is checked during the process with the bore gauge until proper size is reached.

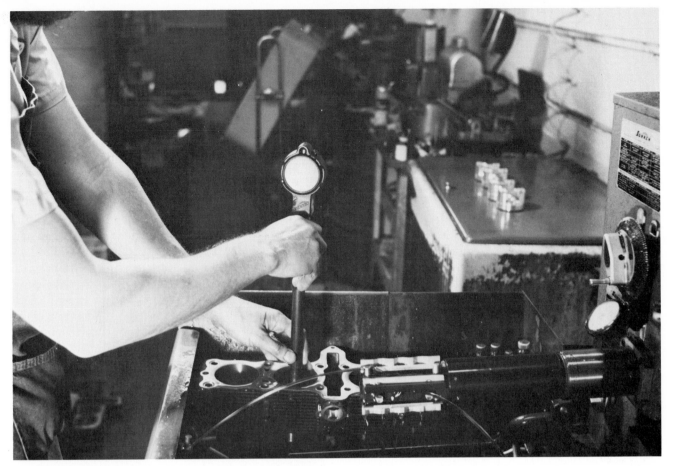

The cylinder bore dimension is checked with a bore gauge during honing until material has been removed to size.

have been established and should be used as guidelines. In the case of aftermarket connecting rods, a clearance callout will be included in the instructions.

All parts that make up the lower end should be Magnafluxed before assembly, even the main-bearing case bolts. This process will detect any cracks or imperfections in these parts. The price of the Magnaflux is cheap insurance against the cost of what can happen when a crankshaft or rod lets go at speed.

The Magnaflux method for ferrous materials such as steel can be summed up as follows. The part is magnetized and covered with a fine magnetic powder. In the vicinity of a crack there is a disturbance of the magnetic flux, and the magnetic powder gathers there, effectively marking the crack.

Cases, crankshafts and rods are coded at the factory with letters and numbers described in the service manual of the particular brand. Combinations of these letters and numbers will give a general idea as to the size bearing that will be needed, but the final sizes will be determined by measurements made with precision measuring instruments.

The crankshaft journals are measured with a micrometer and the readings are noted. Write down the readings in order with cylinder numbers: 1-2-3-4-5 mains, 1-2-3-4 rods, and so on.

The engine cases are assembled with the largest available bearing inserts. The main-journal bolts are torqued to service manual specifications. Use a good assembly lube on the main bolts so that an accurate torque reading will be obtained. Use the same lube when assembling the rods.

With the micrometer set at the reading from crankshaft journal number one, set the bore gauge using the micrometer as a standard. Measure the number one main bearing with the bore gauge. The bore gauge will indicate the clearance between the crank journal and the main bearing. Repeat several times to make sure the readings are correct. Remember, we are dealing with tiny numbers here and it is important that the correct readings are established.

Repeat the procedure on main journals two, three and four. If the clearances are too great on any journal, then smaller size bearings will be needed.

The same procedure is used on the rod bearings. Be sure to use assembly lube on the rod bolts. This is also a good time to check for rod-bolt stretch, which is described later.

One final note. When doing this procedure, it is important that all parts be clean and that it be done in a clean environment.

Connecting rods

There is probably no component in any internal combustion engine that will cause more damage than the failure of a connecting rod! I mean *real damage*. Aside from a connecting rod failing from poor design or metallurgy which is common, let's take a look at the rod bolt, an often overlooked item that even in the case of a high-performance rod can be the weak link. Something as simple as a threaded fastener can cause disaster!

The name Carrillo has been a familiar name in racing for many years. The firm manufactures forged chromoly rods and has a reputation well known in auto racing. Buy a set of Yoshimura rods for a GSXR750 and what do you get? Carrillo.

Included with any new set of rods is an instruction sheet with details on how to torque and measure rod-bolt stretch. As a rod bolt is torqued to its recommended value, it also stretches or becomes longer—about 0.006 to 0.008 in. longer. Now you can almost depend on the quality of the rod bolts of a manufacturer like Carrillo, but there is always a chance that a bad bolt can slip through any quality control system. So by checking rod-bolt stretch you have the last say. If there is any variance in the specifications, then replace the rod bolt.

When torquing a rod bolt or any bolt for that matter, consistency is very important. You should have a recently calibrated torque wrench. I prefer the clicker type. Lubricate the rod bolts with a good high-pressure lubricant.

Using a pin-type micrometer, measure the stretch of the rod bolt at the required torque value. If there is a discrepancy, then you may have a suspect rod bolt. Replace it.

There is something else that I would like to point out in the bolt-torquing procedure. Have you ever noticed a little paint splotch on a bolt in various places on a motorcycle? This is a way of marking a fastener after it has been torqued. On a motorcycle there are plenty of bolts to be torqued so it is easy to forget one now and again. Torquing the rod bolts and main caps—or any bolt for that matter—is very important. Having a check system like the paint method is a good practice when assembling an engine.

Fitting the rod bearings is another important operation. The proper clearance on rod bearings is critical—any good engine builder will testify to this. Checking the rod bearing to crankshaft journal clear-

Just to make sure the size is right, the piston-to-wall clearance is checked with a feeler gauge.

The craftsman and the finished product!

ance is also of utmost importance. Having the proper tools is a necessity. Checking clearances with Plastigauge is all right for general purposes, but not for high-performance applications. The use of precision measuring instruments is also a must. To my friends I will gladly loan my measuring tools, knowing the importance of properly setting the clearances of the lower end of a racing motorcycle engine.

Pistons

In 1975 the Honda 500 and 550 four became a popular motorcycle. I purchased a 550 basket case from a friend and proceeded to rebuild it my own way. At the time there was not much available in the way of performance parts. There were the usual aftermarket pipes, cams and piston kits. Using modified pistons from the Honda CB750 put the displacement up to 591 cc. The only problem was that the dome of the CB750 was not sufficient to bring the compression ratio up to 11.75:1, which is what I wanted. Nor would the aftermarket piston kits. The cylinder head can only be milled so much before you're into the valve seats. After a trip to the local Honda parts department I discovered that the piston of a Honda CB750F had a dome that was a full millimeter higher than the CB750. After reshaping the dome and valve pocket area, I checked the displacement and found that I was at 11.75:1 on the compression ratio.

Aftermarket piston kits will not necessarily give the compression ratio that you might want, only the

potential. The cylinder head almost always must be machined to achieve the desired increase in compression. But this, along with the addition of a higher-lift camshaft, can create problems with valve-to-piston clearance. Piston manufacturers must protect themselves from this possibility by selling pistons that will be easily installed. Then it is up to the individual to do what is necessary to bring compression up to a competitive level.

The ideal would be to have pistons that are finished except for the dome and valve pocket area. This would enable the motorcycle engine builder to custom-machine pistons to his or her specifications. A costly and time-consuming operation, but sometimes necessary.

Piston clearance

When installing new pistons there are a few things to check and do. The cylinder must be bored to the proper dimension. I cannot overemphasize the importance of proper cylinder boring. Too little clearance can lead to piston seizure. Too much clearance can cause the piston to rock in the bore, causing piston slap and poor ring seal.

The area above the top ring on the piston should never contact the cylinder. Unfortunately this cannot be determined unless the engine has been assembled and run for awhile. An engine that is being used for racing should, after an initial run in, be disassembled so things can be checked. If all looks well it may be good for the rest of the season. A properly built Suzuki

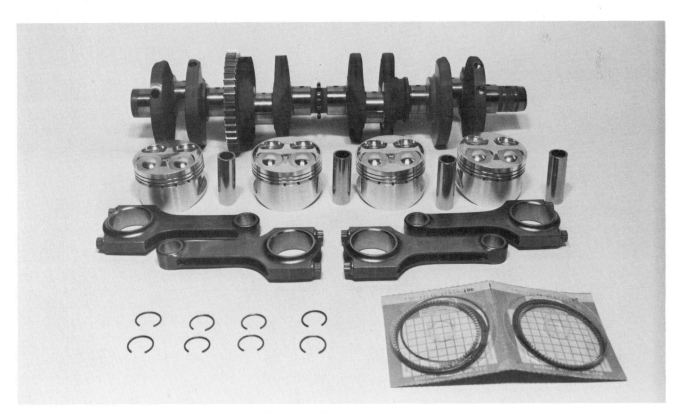

Starting the season with a new crankshaft, Carrillo rods and Cosworth pistons.

GSXR750 engine should be good for at least 2,000 to 3,000 racing miles. I have seen this in a friend's engine that ran a pretty full racing schedule in 1986 and 1987.

Deck height

The outer diameter or the area of the piston that forms the squish area should not rise above the deck or top surface of the cylinder, but as a rule of thumb should be about 0.01 in. below the cylinder. In some cases this can be adjusted by different-thickness base gaskets if available, or the cylinder must be decked or milled by a machine shop. If the desk height is excessively low, this will give away valuable compression. If the piston is too high above the deck, there is a risk due to rod stretch at high rpm that the piston may contact the cylinder head.

Piston-to-pin fit

The piston pin should float in the piston and rod. A basic test that is used is simply to pass the pin into the piston, making sure the pin and piston bores are clean. Turn the piston so that the pin is pointing down. The pin should fall out from its own weight. If it does not, check for burrs in the piston bore. Try this procedure again. If the pin will not fall out, it's too tight. Take the pistons to a machine shop and have them

honed until the pin will fall through. This applies to the top end bearing of the connecting rod as well.

Valve pockets

Having proper valve-to-piston clearance is extremely important. With any engine, having a valve contact the piston can be a disaster, to say the least. When building a high-performance engine, components in the combustion chamber begin to crowd one another and it is necessary to check valve-to-piston clearance to see that there is sufficient room for these parts to coexist. Valve-to-piston clearance is checked at the position of valve overlap. This is the point at which the intake and exhaust valves are open at the same time, just after top dead center. Use a thin layer of modeling clay to cover the top of the pistons with the cylinder head and gasket in place. Push the valves down by hand until they contact the piston. This will leave an impression in the clay. Remove the cylinder head and check the impression in the clay to see that there is enough clearance on the diameter of the valve pocket to accept the valve. About 0.04 in. per side is good. If there is proper clearance, go through the procedure again only this time the camshafts are to be installed. The cams should be within a few degrees of

Main and rod journals are measured with a micrometer and the readings are noted. These readings will be used later to set the bore gauge.

where they will run, and proper valve-to-cam clearances should be close. This check will determine if the depth of the valve pocket is sufficient. About 0.04 to 0.06 in. is good. If on disassembly there is not proper clearance, then the valve pockets must be reworked, or the valves will need sinking into the head.

If the valve pockets are to be reworked, the machinist will need a reference point in the valve pocket. With the cylinder head and gasket, less valves, in place, a transfer punch the size of the valve stem is pushed into the valve guides until it contacts the piston, making a mark that determines the center of the valve pocket. A machinist will pick up this mark to center a cutter used for modifying the valve pockets.

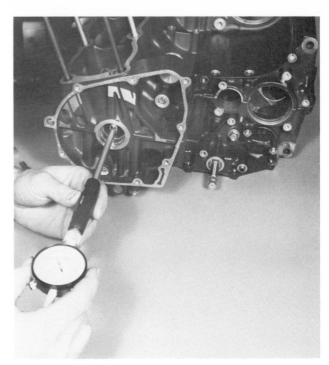

The main bearing journals are measured with the bore gauge. The bore gauge will show a negative reading, which is the bearing-to-journal clearance.

When all modifications to the pistons are complete, be sure that all sharp edges on the dome of the piston are broken. This can be done with a deburring knife and some sandpaper. This operation will take care of any potential hot spots during the combustion cycle.

Ring gap and spacing

Check the ring gap of each set of piston rings by placing them individually in the cylinder they will be run in. Square the gap by pushing the ring down about

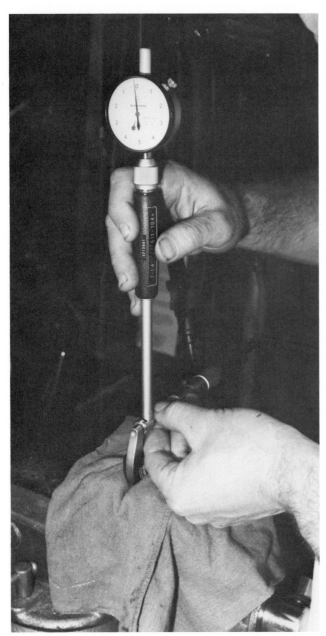

The reading from the main journals are set on the micrometer. The micrometer is then used as a standard for setting the bore gauge.

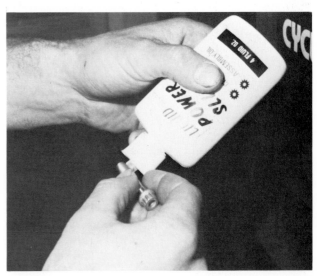

Assembly lube is used on case journal bolts as well as rod bolts so that an accurate torque reading will be obtained.

Torque all rod bolts and case bolts with bearing inserts. Proceed with measurements.

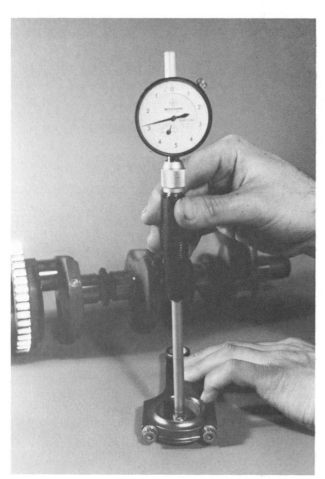

With the rod bearing installed and rod bolts lubed and torqued, a measurement is made with the bore gauge.

a half an inch with the top of the piston. With a feeler gauge, check the end gap clearance to be sure it is within the tolerance callout found in the service manual.

If the gap is too tight, there is a risk of breaking the piston ring. The gap can be increased with a small Carborundum stone or with a tool that is designed for that purpose. Position the rings on the piston according to the specifications in the service manual. Gaps are usually placed at 120 degrees apart on a three-ring piston.

The balancing act

"It is a fact that $1/4$ ounce of unbalance 4 in. from the center of a rotating element creates forces of unbalance equal to 112 Pounds at 8000 RPM." This statement is part of an ad printed by the Stewart–Warner division that manufactures engine-balancing equipment. Just think about what effect that can have on a four-cylinder motorcycle engine that can easily turn 11,500 rpm or more in a racing application!

Before going to an engine-balancing facility, have the crankshaft, connecting rods and pins Magnafluxed. Also, the aluminum pistons should be Zygloed to check for cracks and imperfections. It makes no sense to process engine parts that are rejects. The cost of Magnaflux and Zyglo is economical compared to the cost of replacing a complete engine due to a faulty part.

The Zyglo method for non-ferrous materials such as aluminum can be summed up as follows. The part is immersed in a special activated penetrating oil and viewed under black light.

If the engine being built is going to be used for racing and the generator is removed, there is an oil hole that must be plugged. I prefer the welding-over method using a driven plug. This way the plug cannot fall out. If necessary, the weld can be drilled out.

The balancing procedure starts by weighing pistons with pins and rods to find the lightest of the lot. Pistons and pins are matched by weight by removing material in areas that will not reduce the strength of the piston.

Connecting rods are matched by first making the rotating, or big ends, the same weight. Then the reciprocating, or small ends, are matched for weight. This is done on a scale using a fixture designed for this purpose. If necessary, material is removed from connecting rods by grinding.

On a transverse four-cylinder engine, such as a GSXR750, there is no need to include bearing inserts, piston rings or piston pin clips in the balancing process. These parts are small and usually consistent in weight.

The crankshaft is rotated on the balancing machine at about 600 rpm. The left end of the crankshaft is balanced, then the right end. If the counterweight is heavy on one side of the crankshaft, it is placed in a drill press fixture that locates the center of the crank-

shaft with the center of the drill press spindle. A hole is drilled to remove the proper amount of material from the counterweight to balance the crankshaft. If the counterweights are light, it will be necessary to add weight. In this case the counterweights are drilled from the side and filled with HD-17 heavy metal or Mallory Metal as it is called. This material has a high content of tungsten, weighing two times that of the material that makes up the crankshaft.

The final operation on the crankshaft is the micropolishing of all the journals.

The engine parts Dan O'Donnell was working on were for a Suzuki GSXR750 that will be used for local club racing and AMA Superbike racing. The crankshaft was new and perfectly balanced right out of the box. The Carrillo rods and Cosworth pistons were all within one gram of each other. I did not know this go-

The piston is marked while installed in the motor at the position of valve overlap. The correct position is when both intake and exhaust valves are open the same amount at the same time. Using a transfer punch made from an old valve, push the transfer punch down the valve guide against the piston. Each pocket on each piston is marked using the same procedure. The pistons are removed and placed on a fixture at an angle equal to the valve angle. Using a pointer in the mill the punch mark is located, which centers the valve pocket to the mill.

When torquing the rod bolts during bearing setup, it is a good idea to check the rod bolt stretch with a pin micrometer. If the bolts do not come to the standards set by the manufacturer, then replace the bolt and proceed with setting up the rod bearings.

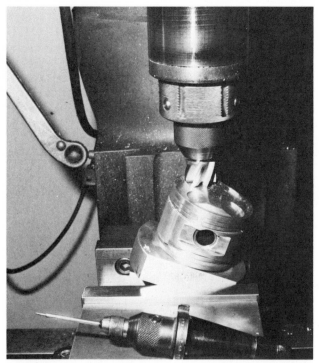

The proper cutter size is chosen and cuts are made to the diameter and depth in each valve pocket. When machining is done, all sharp edges around the valve pockets should be removed with a deburring knife.

The relation between the valves and pockets in the dome of the piston is an important one. When the valves are installed in the cylinder head they will have 0.04 in. clearance per side on the diameter of the valve, and the same clearance between the face of the valve and the pocket in the piston.

ing in, but it speaks well of the quality of the components used in this instance, and I was assured of a well-balanced engine.

There has always been talk about lightening, polishing and knife-edging crankshafts. If you have the money and the time go ahead, but you might be surprised that the guy that beat you at the last race did not go to the trouble. Maybe he has learned to put his time, energy and money to some better use. But then again, that's racing.

Oil and the oiling system

Wars are started over oil. I have listened to many conversations about which oil is best or which viscos-

ity is best and even which brand is best. Synthetic or petroleum? My conclusion is that it is better to use *any* oil than no oil at all.

In the early days of Superbike racing, Keith Code received sponsorship from Golden Spectro Lubricants. The product was one of the first synthetic lubricants directed at the motorcycle market. Many hours on the Axtell dyno showed little if any significant wear on components of the Kawasaki engines being tested. Was this the results of the use of synthetic lubricants or just good design and metallurgy on the part of the Japanese engineers? I may never know and I do not re-

ally care, because the service that I have experienced both on the street and racetrack lead me to believe that any oil is better than no oil. But I do tend to lean toward synthetic oils. I use them in my street motorcycles, and I recommend them for the racing machines of the people that I work with. Let's not forget castor and castor-base oils which have been around for a long time and are still used, particularly in two-stroke racing engines.

Economics are an important consideration in the choice of engine oil. The price of good petroleum-base oil is considerably less compared to the price of synthetic oils. On the other hand, it may not be necessary to change oil as often as I see some people do with synthetic oils. In a street machine, I think you may opt to use synthetic oil and run it 4,000 to 5,000 miles as opposed to petroleum-base oils which people tend to change at say 2,000 miles. So it can be a tradeoff economically. The engine-oil business is competitive, and these people cannot afford a bad product for street or racing. Just a thought: when you buy oil for your street or racer, support the brands that support the sport.

In a racing situation I prefer to change oil and filter after every race. Nobody ever said racing was cheap.

The chance that the oil is that dirty or overused is unlikely, but by studying the metallic particle content of the oil, you can get an idea of the extent of wear inside the engine from the last race. Keep in mind that oil does not wear out, it just gets dirty and contaminated.

My only comment on oil filters is replace them with oil changes and OEM replacements. Beware of cheap imitations!

Oil pumps

I never seem to hear much conversation about that little, out-of-sight mechanical device called the oil pump. Without the oil pump the engine would fry itself in short time.

The oil pumps used by motorcycle manufacturers are of the trochoid type. They consist of two multi-toothed vanes in an aluminum housing. The inner rotor is driven by the engine. Oil is picked up from the sump through a screen and fed to the engine at a pressure regulated by the pressure relief valve. At a designated pressure, a spring compresses in the relief valve and unneeded oil vents back into the oil sump. This pressure relief valve is also an important item and should be looked at on occasion. Oil pressure should be checked once in a while to see that pressure figures

The crankshaft is turned at a low speed by a motor-driven leather belt on a Stewart-Warner balancing machine.

If the crankshaft is out of balance, it is placed on a fixture on a drill press and material is removed by drilling until the correct balance is achieved.

When the crankshaft has been balanced the journals are polished, ready for assembly.

are within the specifications called out by the manufacturer.

The pickup screen is another out-of-sight out-of-mind item that should be inspected once in a while. It can be clogged to the point of cutting oil flow to the pump. I would especially recommend inspection of the oil pump after the break-in period of a new motorcycle. I have found a good amount of case sealing material in some screens. The fact that not much is heard about the oil pump system speaks well about its reliability, but keep an eye on the oiling system.

Oil coolers

Suzuki Motorcycle Company, on the GSXR series motorcycle, has certainly proved that oil cooling works. It will be interesting to see if and when Suzuki will turn to water cooling.

Motorcycles such as the Honda VFR750, Yamaha FZR750 and other water-cooled models are also fitted with oil coolers. Something unique about these latter oiling systems is that the oil pumps are two-staged. Actually they are two pumps in one. One stage, the larger, feeds the engine while the smaller stage feeds the oil cooling system. The second stage pumps oil through a cooler, then back into the system. This is a safer, more efficient way to cool oil than having a cooler off the main oiling system. For racing applica-

Connecting rods are balanced end for end and then to an overall equal weight. This is done on a scale specially designed for that purpose.

Pistons and pins are measured and matched for weight. Rings and pin keepers need not be measured, as these parts are small and usually consistent in weight.

tions it may be a good idea to increase the size of the oil cooler if excessive oil temperatures are experienced. Production units are designed for production use, but not for serious competition.

Suzuki GSXR750 and GSXR1100 motorcycles can be equipped with an additional oil cooler that cools the oil to the top end. The line from the back of the case feeds into the oil cooler which is placed up front in the fairing. The cooler outlet line is split and feeds into special fittings attached to the rocker cover. Yamaha and Honda supply larger coolers with their race kits.

Under racing conditions, oil should be kept at about 190-210 degrees Fahrenheit. Oil temperature any higher should be an issue of concern.

A good source for oil coolers and plumbing is Earl's Supply in Carson, California. Another good source would be a unit from Lockhart.

Mounting the oil cooler up front will require the services of a good metal fabricator. The cooler needs to be placed in an area with good air circulation.

If the engine is to be run in a racing class that allows the removal of armature, the hole in the end of the crankshaft should be welded closed.

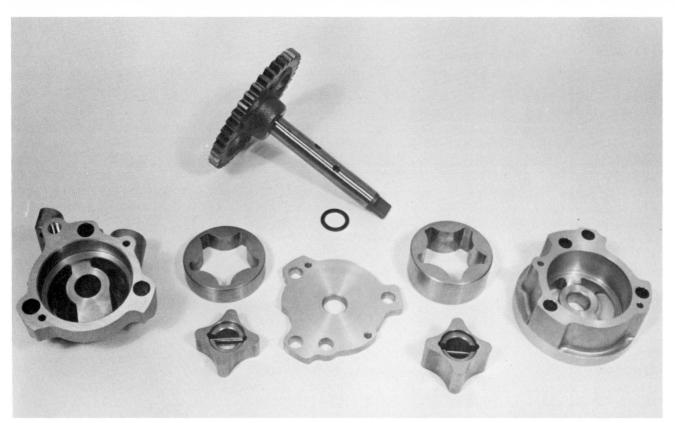

The disassembled oil pump is a typical trochoid system used by most motorcycle manufacturers today. The smaller stage feeds the oil cooler and the larger stage feeds the engine. This particular unit is from a Yamaha FZR750.

At top is the Lockhart oil cooler, a very high quality product available in kit form for most motorcycles. On bottom is one of the oil coolers available from Earl's Supply. This unit has been used in car racing for years and comes in many sizes.

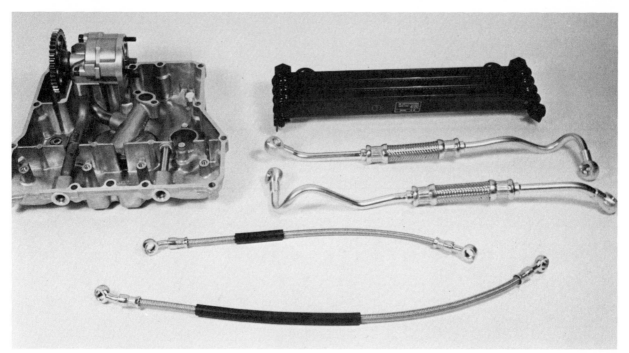

The complete two-stage oil system from a Yamaha FZR750 includes pump, special oilpan, oil cooler and oil lines. The two flexible lines at the bottom of the photo are for the top end oil feed system. The system will bolt right to my FZR1000.

Here is a collection of petroleum products that I've collected at my shop and in the garage at home. I have used all of these and some others. I would like to suggest that when you purchase petroleum products or any product related to motorcycles, do give consideration to companies and products that support the sport of motorcycling.

Chapter 8

Gearing; gearbox, clutch and chain

Tuning a motorcycle is not limited to the engine. One of the simplest ways to increase performance is by changing gear ratios. Production motorcycles tend to be geared on the high side and with good reason. These motorcycles are used for the street with a good portion of the miles put on just riding from here to there on freeways.

Say you are cruising along at 55 mph and the tachometer is reading 3800 rpm. If you were to add maybe three teeth to the rear sprocket and bump that 3800 rpm tach reading up to say 4200 rpm at 55 mph, what do you suppose will happen? It's going to accelerate quicker! Your buddy next to you is going to wonder what has happened when you just roll away on a

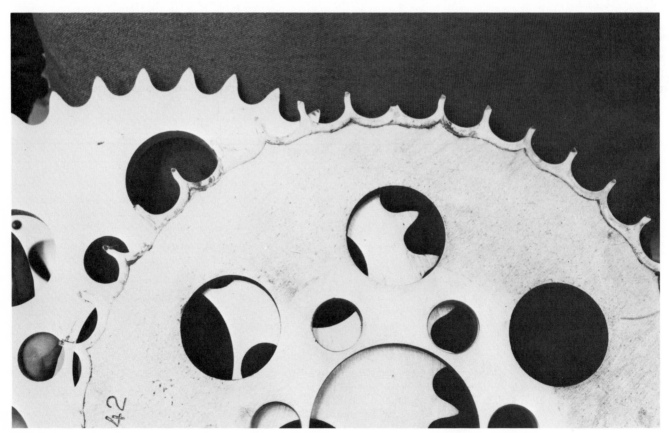

An example of a well-used rear sprocket. Even with some teeth missing the sprocket survived the trip home.

friendly acceleration contest. Remember that you will be giving something away. The motor is buzzing at a higher rpm now. Some gas mileage is lost, the engine is wearing a bit faster and your friend is not happy about being outrun. But the motorcycle performs better with a small amount of time and money invested.

On the racetrack, gearing is a very important tuning area and the tuner must be aware of the particular racetrack layout in order to gear the motorcycle for optimum performance. Gearing for Daytona Speedway will be much different than gearing for Sears Point International Raceway. Keep in mind that an engine can pull only so many rpm. That rpm should be kept in its optimum power range during the lap around the track. Getting a good drive out of high-speed turns is more important, maybe, than hitting the rev-limiter down the straightaway or smoking the tire out of the tightest turn on the racetrack.

To calculate gear ratios it is necessary to know the primary, secondary and gearbox ratios for the particular engine being used. This information can be found in the data portion of the service manual for that particular motorcycle.

Other considerations are tire size and its rolling distance; the distance covered by the rear tire for one

With some aluminum tubing and plate stock a stand can be fabricated for keeping sprockets in good order.

Changing gear ratios with a chain-drive system is a snap when you consider what Dr. John has to go through to make a gear change on his winning Moto Guzzi with its shaft drive.

The Honda VF1000R five-speed gearbox looks like just about every current Japanese motorcycle gearbox—except that this gearbox could probably hold up in a Ford automobile as well.

revolution. Remember the tire will "grow" at higher speeds and there will be a loss due to some slippage. Keep a record of ratios used at different tracks and try new combinations during practice sessions.

The street rider can add two or three teeth to the rear sprocket to get the engine to pull maximum rpm in high gear. The increased acceleration out of your favorite canyon turn will impress you!

The gearbox

I would like to think there is an area in a motorcycle engine that needs no attention. The gearbox comes close.

The stock gearbox in the average high-performance motorcycle today will give good service for many miles. When the motorcycle is used for box stock racing its service time decreases. If the engine output is increased this puts an even higher load on the gearbox components.

In a racing situation, shifting without using the clutch is common practice; racers often just let off on the throttle a bit to unload the gearbox. Under these conditions the shifting dogs must mate into their positions to make the gear change. These mating parts get worn in the process and can allow the gearbox to jump out of gear. This is where the racing gearbox comes in. In order to keep the cost of production down, gearboxes may have gears that are cast, then machined and hardened—mass production.

The racing gearbox

A good racing gearbox will be made from high quality billet steel that is machined and heat treated. The result is a much stronger gearbox along with a much higher price tag. These units are generally six-speed and close-ratio.

Six-speed gearboxes shift better, too. The gears are narrower, to fit the extra gear into the engine cases.

The term "back cutting the gearbox" really means back cutting the shifting dogs. Notice the slight negative angle on the shift dog on the gear in the photo. The gear came this way from the factory, and when the gear is under a load this angle provides a mechanical advantage when engaged to help keep the set of gears in that gear position.

The gears don't have to travel as far to engage and the shift drum has one more detent position so it rotates less between shifts. Some manufacturers having racing departments may offer optional ratios for these gearboxes.

Periodic inspection of the gearbox is a good idea. At this time, parts should be checked for wear and should measure within the tolerances called for by the manufacturer. If parts pass this test, they should go through Magnaflux inspection. This will show any fractures or imperfections invisible to the human eye. The inspection is worth the time and money. I have seen two recent situations where gears have split in two; one came out through the top of the engine case causing major damage.

Another area to inspect is the shifting mechanism, including the shift drum, forks and shafts. Next, check any linkage that operates the shift drum. There are springs and pins in these systems, any one of which can break and leave the gearbox locked in gear.

For gearbox shimming, the best practice is simply to follow the manufacturers' specifications.

Special gear coatings are available. My philosophy is: If you have the extra money, go ahead. Just keep in mind that you are going to run oil in that gearbox and it is still the best lubricant between metal parts.

The clutch

The dry clutch has been used for many years in two-stroke Grand Prix racers. The engines develop power at high rpm, and with this narrow power band the clutch takes some incredible abuse at the starting line and up until the motorcycle reaches a speed that matches that power band. In the smaller-class racers, the clutch could be used like another gear coming out of tight turns where rpm drop below the power band.

One area of the gearbox to pay special attention to is the actual shifting mechanism that rotates the shift drum. Compared to the rest of the gearbox this system is rather fragile looking. There are a number of small springs, pins and detents that can break, any one of which will leave the gearbox stranded in the last gear it was in. If this happens in a race it's all over for the event. If this happens on the road let's hope that your auto club card is still valid—or a good friend has a van!

Here is one of those items that needs to be paid attention to when assembling a gear. With oil-feed gearboxes in motorcycles today, any splined bushings or sleeves with oil holes should be lined up with the corresponding oil holes in the mainshaft and output shafts.

The ability to slip the dry clutch is probably its best characteristic. The dry clutch has a very positive feel about it, whereas a wet clutch seems a bit mushy. The friction material of a dry clutch plate is hard compared to the softer cork-like material found in the wet clutch. The wet clutch gives a soft feel and it can require more effort to find that optimum position for a great charge off the line. In the early days of Superbikes with the larger 1000 cc engines, the riders had enough torque to drop the clutch and smoke the tire off the line!

The fact is that a dry clutch, with its hard-compound friction plates, requires less movement to disengage the clutch. And so the clutch lever ratio can be rather low, also giving a better feel to the system. On a wet system with soft friction plates, more throw is needed to disengage the clutch. Some years ago, when it was necessary to use stiffer springs in a wet clutch to make it stand up, the rider also had to sit in front of the TV at night with a hand exerciser to develop muscles strong enough to pull in the clutch lever. I did it just so I could go on the Sunday ride with the guys.

The Japanese manufacturers realized the need for stronger clutches as engine output increased. They also confronted the problem of how to actuate the clutch. Enter the hydraulic clutch actuating system, HCAS. That wouldn't look good as a decal on the side of a motorcycle and that is probably why it's not seen. Anyway, with hydraulic systems, we don't have to exercise our left hands anymore to get through the Sunday ride. Now if you are going racing, it might be a good idea to exercise both hands because on a race course it will be necessary to do some serious hanging on!

The most important advantage of the hydraulic system is that it allows the use of higher spring pressure in the clutch system eliminating slippage under power, yet with hydraulic assist it becomes easier for the rider to use. So unless you have a great excess of money in the riding or racing budget for a dry clutch, don't sell short the current wet clutch systems.

Clutch plate stack

It is important that the thickness of the clutch plates are within the specifications supplied by the manufacturer. If the pack is under proper dimension, the spring pressure will be less and the clutch will be more prone to slippage.

Clutch plate warpage

The steel plates can warp if overheated. They should be checked on a flat surface plate and replaced

The clutch assembly from a Honda VF1000R shows the reinforcing ring around the outer clutch hub. Two other items are unique to the Honda clutch. The first is the sprag clutch inside the inner hub. This allows the clutch and rear wheel to freewheel, lessening the chance of locking or chattering of the rear tire while decelerating under engine compression. The second is the diaphragm-type clutch spring.

if not flat. A good economy surface plate is a piece of 1/4 inch plate glass cut to about twelve by sixteen inches and available from a glass supply source. This glass plate also provides a good surface for lapping by covering it with a sheet of sandpaper.

If the steel plates are flat but have surface glaze, the plates can be glass-bead blasted and reused. The bonded friction plates should be replaced if not up to the standards in the service manual.

Clutch springs

The most common spring is the wire wound type. Honda, on its Intercepter series, uses a disc- or diaphragm-type spring. This system works very well with the higher-torque V-4 engines.

There is not much that can be done to increase the spring pressure. Wound springs can be replaced with higher-pressure aftermarket units or can even be shimmed with thin steel washers for extra pressure.

Clutch adjustment

The hydraulic clutch is self adjusting, another nice advantage of the unit. Keep the fluid reservoir topped off and see to it that the system is properly bled. Otherwise the system is almost maintenance-free.

Cable-operated clutches may have two adjustment points, one at the handlebar and, sometimes, one at the engine. Check the particular make and model for location of the adjuster. If there is an adjuster it may need some clearance between the clutch rod and actuator.

With hydraulic clutches there is no cable to maintain, but on the clutch there is still a barrel that rotates in the clutch lever. That barrel and the pivot bolt can use some lubrication from time to time; this goes for the lever pivot bolt on the front brake master cylinder, too. I suggest some white lithium grease that is packaged in a spray can.

While servicing in this area, check to see that all cables and fluid lines are clear of being pinched between the triple clamps or fork tubes and the frame.

The chain game

How would you like to be someone else's motorcycle chain? I think I have read and heard just about everything concerning this piece of equipment. From this gossip and many miles on a motorcycle, both racing and street, I have developed some pretty strong opinions. I used to wonder why Jody Nicholas could easily get 20,000 miles out of a chain, back when they didn't make 20,000 mile chains. Nicholas frequently washed the chain in cleaning solvent, let it soak for a day or so in a pan of oil and then hung it up to drip dry! His secret was periodic maintenance.

Talking recently with a friend who had purchased a new chain (guaranteed for 25,000 miles), he informed me that he had gotten only 5,000 miles of service from this new chain. He called the supplier, told him the problem and he sent him a new chain. I hope

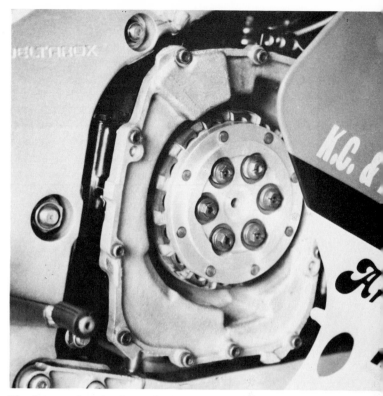

The factory dry clutch on the Yamaha FZR750 ridden by Ritchie Arnaiz. The clutch hub sits well inboard of the cases allowing the use of the shorter-type gearbox mainshaft.

this time he gets what was advertised, or at least he gets three more free chains!

We are well into the era of the O-ring chain, and I think it does very well. My last chain which was original equipment on my VF1000F Honda lasted 24,000 miles. Pretty impressive! I think I could have gotten another 3,000 miles if it had not been for riding two days in the rain in Minnesota, while coming home after spending the weekend at the AMA National road races in Elkhart Lake, Wisconsin.

My point is there is nothing that will destroy a motorcycle chain quicker than water, yet I see people in the five-minute car wash putting high-pressure water and strong detergent to their chains. If your motorcycle is so dirty that it requires the five-minute car wash, then save that last worn-out chain and install it just for the car wash—or any wash for that matter. Just keep that good chain away from water if at all possible.

You cannot lubricate the pins and bushing of an O-ring chain! Think about it. It's prelubed and sealed with O-rings. Oiling the chain, however, will keep the rollers lubricated and keep the chain from rusting. I don't clean my chain with any type of solvents. There are additives in solvents and cleaners that can destroy the properties of a rubber O-ring. After oiling my chain, I wipe it with a rag soaked with WD-40 or a similar product. This cleans the excess chain lube off, along with any dirt, and leaves a light protective film of oil that does not sling off.

Chains don't stretch much, aside from a slight initial set in its early life, but they do most certainly wear at the pin-and-bushing area. An old chain can be laid on the floor and fully extended, then compressed. The difference in length tells you how much wear has taken place. As a chain wears, the dimension between the pins and bushings becomes greater and the chain rides higher on the sprocket. The sprockets are designed in a way to compensate for chain wear. A chain is never really worn-out until it breaks or goes beyond the adjustability point where it rides over the sprocket teeth. A worn chain can cause an annoying grinding sound much like that of a damaged wheel bearing. At Daytona in 1987, Jeff Stern pitted with what we thought was an output shaft bearing going out. The problem turned out to be that the chain had thrown three rollers. A much easier fix to say the least!

My choice for the street is definitely an O-ring style chain. A chain used for racing is a different thing, however. First, we are not interested in high mileage; the idea is to finish the race. I do not recommend an O-ring chain for racing. It's more expensive, heavier and

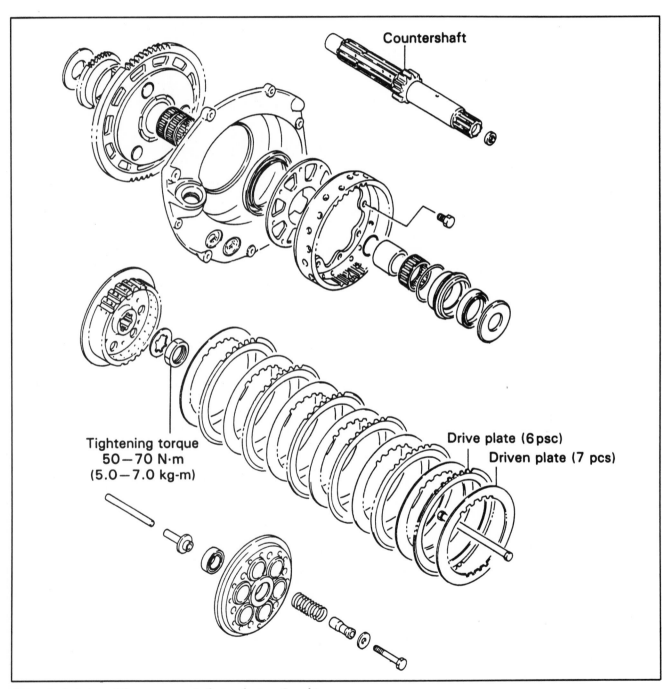

Countershaft

Tightening torque
50—70 N·m
(5.0—7.0 kg-m)

Drive plate (6 psc)
Driven plate (7 pcs)

An exploded view of the components that make up a Suzuki GSXR750 dry clutch assembly. These units are available through Yoshimura R & D. Yoshimura R & D of America

not as flexible as a standard roller chain. The standard roller chain can be cleaned, oiled and used on another race day or most of the season in some cases.

When replacing a motorcycle chain, whether for street or race, remember there are different grades of chain. Use a good name brand from a reliable source in case there is any difficulty with the product. Check with fellow riders to see what is giving good service, and take a little more time to maintain and adjust that often overlooked, unloved motorcycle chain. Also be sure when replacing a chain to use the correct size.

I have tried about everything possible for chain lubrication. How about sealing wax mixed with oil over an open flame in a coffee can? Or a white lithium

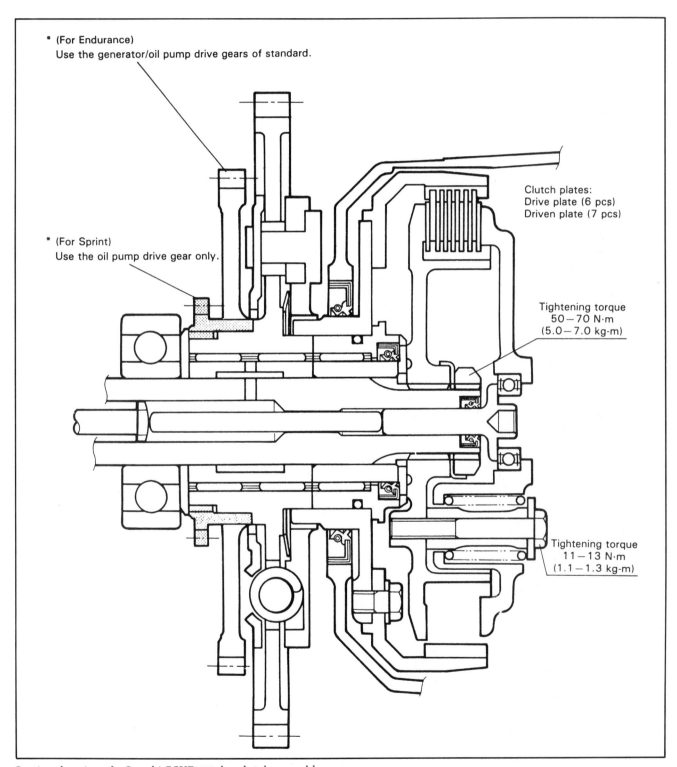

* (For Endurance)
Use the generator/oil pump drive gears of standard.

* (For Sprint)
Use the oil pump drive gear only.

Clutch plates:
Drive plate (6 pcs)
Driven plate (7 pcs)

Tightening torque
50 — 70 N·m
(5.0 — 7.0 kg-m)

Tightening torque
11 — 13 N·m
(1.1 — 1.3 kg-m)

Section drawing of a Suzuki GSXR750 dry clutch assembly.
Yoshimura R & D of America

If weight is a real concern the chain-drive system can be modified for 520 size chain with a roller width of 0.25 versus 530 at 0.375. With the minimum weight of Superbikes at 390 lb. and having to add weight to make the scale it really is questionable to sacrifice the heavier 530 chain.

grease applied by heating the chain with an acetylene torch? Or tallow (animal fat)? Or ninety-weight gear oil thinned with a degreasing agent? *Anything* is better than nothing. Today my choice is PJ1 Blue Label.

The weakest point in a motorcycle chain is in the master link, particularly the clip that holds it together. I used to safety wire them, but with the more rectangular side plates and plastic guides that are on today's motorcycle swing arms, the safety wire would wear through. This is a good place for RTV sealant to hold that master link clip in place. Be sure to clean the side plate with contact cleaner so the RTV will adhere. Make sure the clip is installed in the right direction. There are also master links that, after the side plate is put in place, the pins can be peened over with a hammer. This makes the master link permanent. Not a bad idea on a street motorcycle, but for racing where gear ratio changes will be necessary, I do not recommend the use of the permanent master link. As for street use, you will not be able to remove the chain when washing the motorcycle.

Why with all these maintenance problems do motorcycle manufacturers even bother with link chain? Why not just use shaft-drive systems like certain models do? First, chain is economical to produce. But most of all it is efficient. The percentage of efficiency runs in the high eighties for shaft drive, low nineties for chain and high nineties for belt. So, for touring or sport touring, shaft drives are great, but for street performance and racing where gear ratio changes are necessary and efficiency is a must, roller chain will do just fine.

This Suzuki is equipped with a factory dry clutch assembly. Very nice and very expensive.

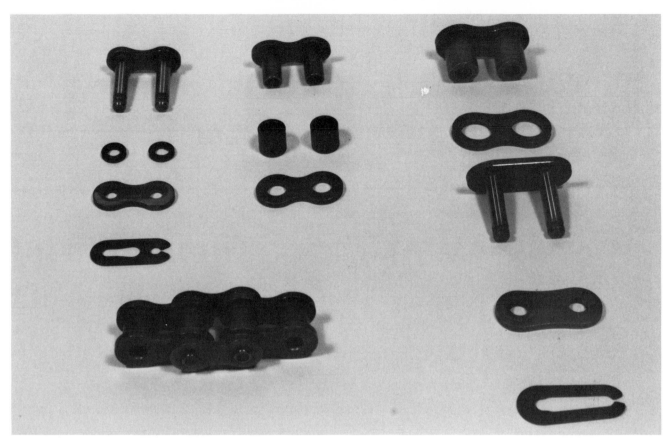

The current 530 O-ring chain versus the old 630 sintered
roller chain.

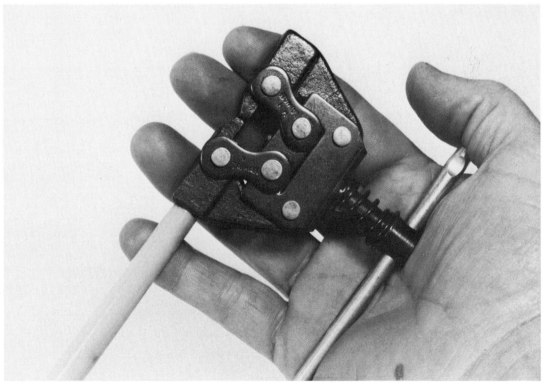

A good chain breaker should be in the motorcyclist's tool-
box.

QR SERIES CHAINS

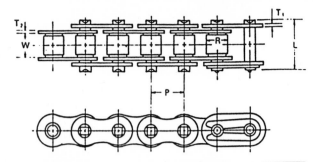

	Pitch	Roller dia.	Roller Link Width	Pin Link Plate Thickness	Roller Link Plate Thickness	Pin length	Ave. Tensile Strength	Weight
	P	R	W	T_1	T_2	L	lbs.	lbs./ft.
420	½	.306	.252	.059	.059	.622	4.180	.40
▲ 428 QR	½	.335	.313	.071	.071	.726	5.280	.54
▲ 520 QR	⅝	.400	.252	.079	.079	.819	7.040	.64
▲ 525 QR	⅝	.400	.313	.079	.079	.823	7.040	.67
▲ 530 QR	⅝	.400	.375	.079	.079	.898	7.040	.70
▲ 630 QR	¾	.469	.375	.094	.094	.976	10.000	.93

Note: Nickel Plated Chains are also available for above chains.
   Chains cut to specific length or on reels are in stock for immediate delivery.
   ▲ Quad staked riveting.

HSL SERIES CHAINS

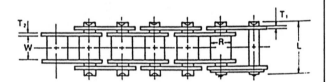

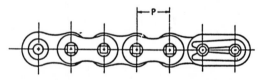

	Pitch	Bushing dia.	Inner Link Width	Pin Link Plate Thickness	Inner Link Plate Thickness	Pin length	Ave. Tensile Strength	Weight
	P	R	W	T_1	T_2	L	lbs.	lbs./ft.
428HSL	½	.335	.313	.059	.079	.772	3.740	0.48
▲ 520HSL	⅝	.400	.252	.079	.110	.850	7.040	0.71
▲ 530HSL	⅝	.400	.375	.079	.110	.972	7.040	0.77
▲ 630HSL	¾	.469	.375	.094	.138	1.075	10.000	1.06

Note: Nickel plated chains are also available for above chains.
   Chains cut to specific length or on reels are in stock for immediate delivery.
   ▲ Quad staked riveting.

Chapter 9

Fast fuel

Street riders have no real need for a drybreak refueling system. It would be rather novel, however, to make a pit stop at the Rock Store some afternoon and have your friends pit you with a six-second fuel stop. Don't laugh. I have seen some pretty novel things go on at motorcycle watering holes on Sunday afternoons!

Fast and safe refueling probably best describes the drybreak system. I remember the day some years ago

Pit stops take time. Here is an example of how Bubba Shobert of Team Honda gets in and out so quickly. Seven people who know what they are doing are seven reasons for a quick pit stop.

Using the drybreak refueling system, the pitman is just removing the fuel container from the motorcycle and the rest of the crew is beginning to push the rider. Aside from being *quick, this system is safe with little or no fuel spillage. Suzuki GSXR1100 Team Hyper Cycle at the 1987 Sears Point National endurance race.*

when Harry Klinzman pitted at Riverside Raceway during the AFM six-hour race and suddenly found himself on fire, along with his motorcycle. Refueling from a regular gas can is dangerous, to say the least.

In professional or club racing where a few extra seconds in the pits can cost a position or two, along with the safety factor, the drybreak proves itself.

The drybreak is not an item that can just be attached to a tank. In this chapter I will go through what is involved in installing a system in a GSXR750 fuel tank.

The drybreak assembly includes the drybreak, O-ring, nine Phillips flathead screws and a weld-ring. The ring must be machined from steel so it can be welded to the tank. The tank being modified will be used in Superbike and endurance events. More fuel capacity will be good, and the removal of the air filter system will allow the fuel tank to be closed off, allowing more capacity. The portion of the tank that surrounds the air cleaner is removed with an abrasive cutting tool. The top of the tank around the stock fuel filler cap is also removed to accept the drybreak weld-ring.

A cardboard pattern is used to make the sheet metal cover to be welded to the bottom of the tank. It is

not really necessary to remove the dome that covers the air filter, but there will need to be some holes made around the perimeter to let the fuel into the compartment when the new bottom is welded in. The drybreak weld-ring is welded in place at the top of the tank.

After welding, the tank should be thoroughly cleaned inside with a metal prep solution and dried out. Before painting, the tank should be treated inside with a slushing compound such as Tank Kreem or a similar slush that is available at aircraft supply stores.

If the racing association that you are competing in has a fuel tank capacity limit and you are over that limit, use pingpong balls to adjust the capacity. Yes, I said pingpong balls!

To complete this fast refueling system, a dump can will be needed that is compatible with the drybreak system in the fuel tank.

The drybreak system will allow safe refueling in about six seconds. That would dazzle the Sunday morning crowd at the local watering hole, but it is a necessity when competing at Daytona Speedway or any track where safe and fast fuel stops are needed.

The drybreak, weld-ring, O-ring and tank bottom. This is the standard setup in the industry.

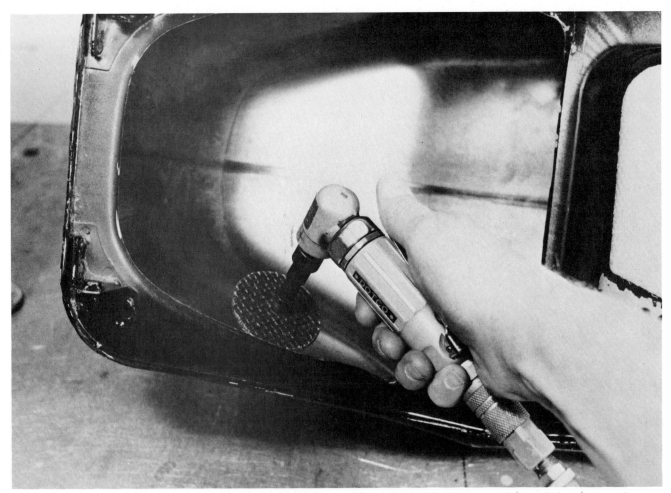

In the case of the Suzuki GSXR, more fuel capacity was needed. The bottom of the tank is removed so that a new bottom can be welded in. Extra fuel capacity may not be needed for sprint racing, but is a definite advantage in endurance racing where the number of fuel stops can significantly affect the outcome of the race.

A cardboard pattern is used to mark the material. The metal is cut out on a band saw.

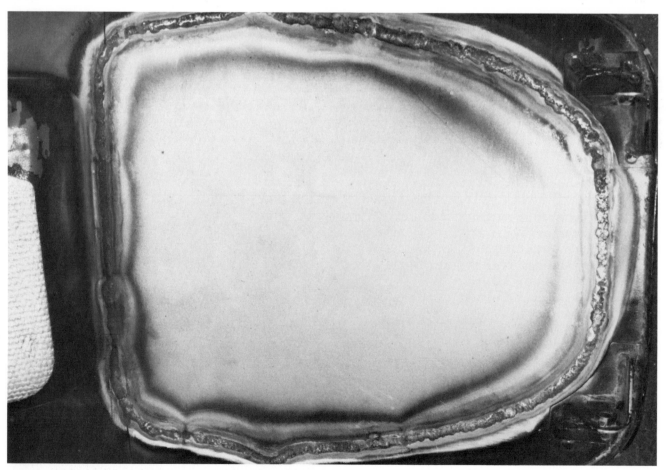

The new bottom is welded onto the bottom of the tank. This can be acetylene gas-welded or done with heli-arc. A heli-arc leaves a cleaner seam.

The weld-ring is machined from 3/16 inch steel and is turned out on the lathe.

Using the drybreak as a pattern, holes are drilled and tapped into the weld-ring.

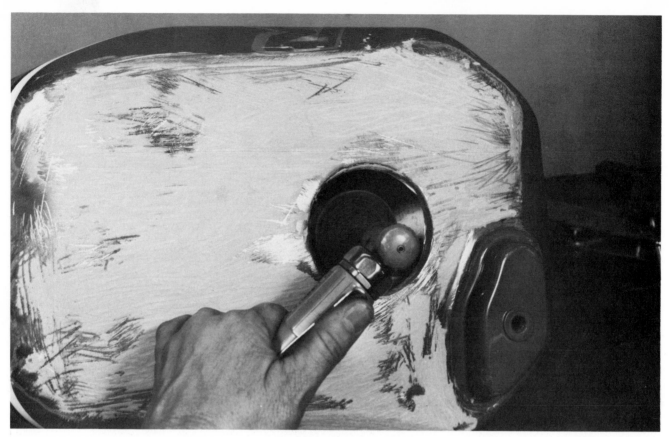

An air grinder is used to remove the old filler cap mounting.

With the weld-ring in place and welded, the tank is ready for painting. The next step is some fast fuel stops.

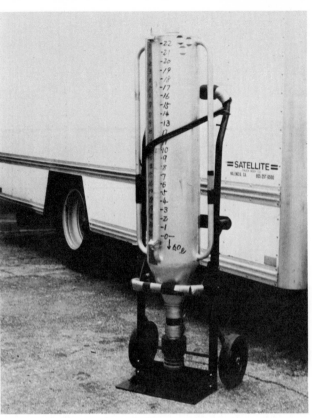

A Pacific Racing dump can with a drybreak head. It's an OK system if you have time to spare. Work continues on an air vent system to allow the fuel to flow faster.

Transporting a dump can to and from the pits stimulates creativity. The modification of a simple dolly was the answer in this case.

Team Honda has a very sophisticated dump can system with an exterior valve that allows air to rapidly escape from the fuel tank as the fuel goes in. It takes about six seconds to fill the tank with this system.

Jeff Stern, right, and Ben Hauffman fuel up prior to the start of 1988 Daytona Superbike race.

Chapter 10

Fasteners and safety wiring

The bolts, screws, nuts and washers supplied by motorcycle manufacturers are of very good quality and more than match the application. Dealer parts departments usually have a pretty good supply of random hardware in the most common sizes. This is a better choice versus the standard hardware store variety.

Stainless-steel fasteners are OK in a situation where corrosion from some element may occur. Com-

When pre-race preparation is complete and all the safety wire pliers, torque wrenches and little bottles of locking compound are put away, the motorcycle must pass through the gauntlet of the tech inspector. This is the last official look at the machine before gridding in a race. Don't ever be too critical of these people if they happen to call you on something: it may be something that could save a rider's life!

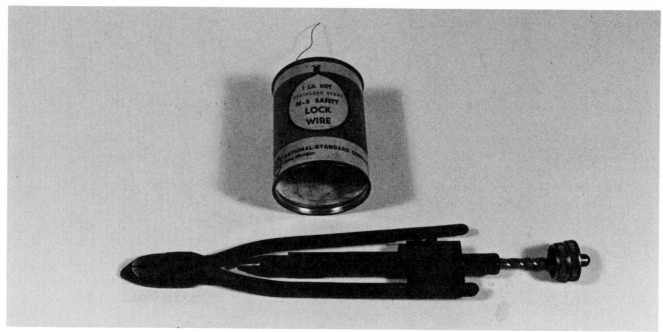

Safety wire pliers and quality wire.

mon stainless-steel fasteners do not have the strength of good steel fasteners, and finding the right sizes may take up time that could be better spent in another area.

If the purchase of extra fasteners is necessary, use the same system, metric or otherwise, so that the same wrenches can be used throughout the project—metric, American standard or Whitworth.

A hose clamp around the oil filter cartridge. The hose clamp can then be safety wired to the engine case.

Safety wiring

Safety wiring is an art. It was developed years ago by the aircraft industry which did not have the locking-type fasteners and agents such as Loctite that are available today. Even with new fastener technology, safety wiring is still used in the aircraft industry. The safety wiring done daily by seasoned aircraft mechanics is truly a work of art; it must be in order to pass inspections. As for motorcycle racing, safety wiring is part of the event.

The tool

There is only one tool needed for safety wiring—the safety wire pliers. The person who developed this tool had just one thing in mind and that was efficiency. I would own a pair of safety wire pliers just for the sake of owning the tool!

The next item you'll need is the wire. Any wire will do, but the real product is the best bet. The dispensing packaging alone is worth the price. There are a number of wire sizes available. I have always preferred the 0.025 in. diameter for my uses. About the only things needed are holes to put the wire through.

I recommend safety wiring only when it is required. I do not see the benefit of wiring every bolt and nut on a motorcycle. I like to stick to the items that are required by the rules of the association that is being raced in. But the bottom line is, if it makes you feel better, then wire it.

Get in the habit of checking any bolt or nut to see that it is tight before safety wiring it. A loose oil line or brake line will not be kept from leaking by safety wire alone. The bolts described may not fall out due to safety wire, but the leakage that may occur can certainly put you on the ground.

Drilling

Drilling a small hole in the head of a bolt or side of a nut can be very frustrating without applying some simple techniques. I have a Bridgeport milling machine which is most handy for safety-wire hole drilling. Now I realize with the cost of racing that a milling machine is probably not in the budget, so let's approach the problem with just a hand drill motor and a bench vise. The drill motor should turn about 1500 rpm. From a machine tool store, buy a package of 0.062 in. diameter cobalt stub drills; the cost is a little higher, but the results are well worth the expense. Higher-quality drills of this type have what is called a split point which helps to keep the drill from wandering. Use a center punch to mark the spot to be drilled, not too big of a punch mark, however, so as not to work-harden the material. The use of a cutting solution such as Tapmatic is a must.

Start drilling, gently! One of the most common mistakes when drilling a hole is trying to force the drill bit to cut faster than it is capable of cutting. After drilling, use a larger drill and carefully deburr the hole on both sides. A sharp edge here can make pulling the wire through the hole difficult and can even cut the safety wire.

When drilling a bolt, drill all the way across the head. When drilling a nut it is necessary to go to the side. There are drilling fixtures available for this operation.

Single wiring

Single wiring is the use of a single strand of safety wire. It is used where access is difficult and may not allow the double-wire method, or where time is short, such as changing a part on the starting line under the five-minute board!

Double wiring

The double-wire method is the most common. It is the most time consuming but the most efficient as well. It takes practice getting the right number of twists between fasteners. Be careful not to overtwist the wire or it will work-harden and break. The idea is to have just enough twist so that when the wire is pulled tight through the next fastener, the twisted part will pull tight, too.

In the aircraft industry there is a rule specifying the number of turns per inch based on the wire diameters and how many fasteners can be wired in a series. The rule allows no more fasteners in a series than can be safety wired by a twenty-four-inch length of wire. The only area on a motorcycle that pertains to this rule

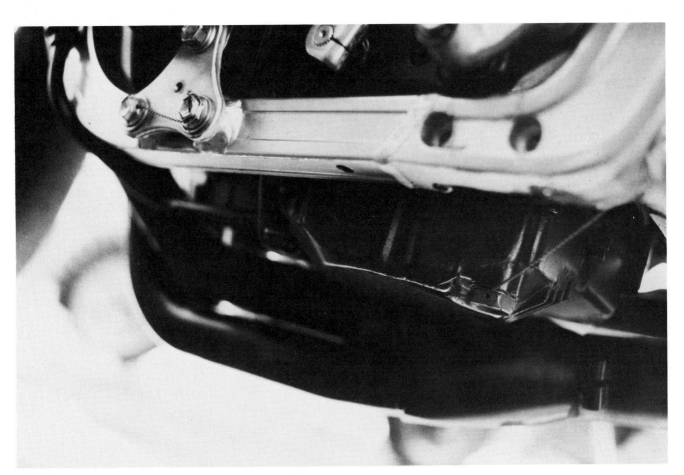

Any fastener that caps or connects a fluid source will need to be safety wired. These are oil and water drain plugs and filler caps.

would be the rear sprocket bolts. Avoid the agony of wrestling a long piece of safety wire by wiring just two at a time. Keep in mind the rotation of the fastener. It should be safety wired so that the wire is pulling in the proper direction.

Never safety wire your tires, knees or any part of the hand. Over the years I have seen people in the pits at races become careless about where they put the cut-off ends of safety wire. These little pieces of wire are razor sharp and if carelessly discarded can find their way into tires and those other unpleasant areas. Please be considerate to yourself and others by placing safety wire trimmings in the trash.

Loctite

While on the subject of securing fasteners, let's talk about a product that will help those nuts and bolts stay where they belong. With the proper torque valve applied to a fastener along with a medium grade of Loctite, such as 242, there should be no worry about the fastener coming loose. Any good shop manual will indicate areas where Loctite should be used.

When using Loctite be sure to know the grade; there are grades that are almost permanent and can only be loosened with heat. Use Loctite sparingly. It doesn't take much more than a drop per fastener.

Loctite is best used where a fastener threads into a threaded blind hole. When a fastener passes through a non-threaded hole and a nut is used, the use of elastic- or steel-type lock nuts is advisable. These types of lock nuts can be reused a number of times. A rule of thumb is that if a lock-type nut can be threaded on a bolt with your fingers then it's time to discard the nut or use Loctite to secure it.

Silicone seal and duct tape

Two items that I see used to secure items on and around motorcycles are silicone seal and duct tape. Silicone seal is for sealing between two surfaces. It can also be used to form a gasket but not for holding fasteners in place. This application is poor engineering at its best; use safety wiring or Loctite products instead. Don't use silicone seal around gasoline as it will never set and could end up in some undesirable places, such as carburetor jets.

Duct tape is a great product for emergencies, such as taping your road race boots so the wind won't come in for the first five feet of the first turn you ride through. I think of duct tape as the absolutely last resort for repairing something on a motorcycle. Keeping that in mind, it becomes a handy item to have around.

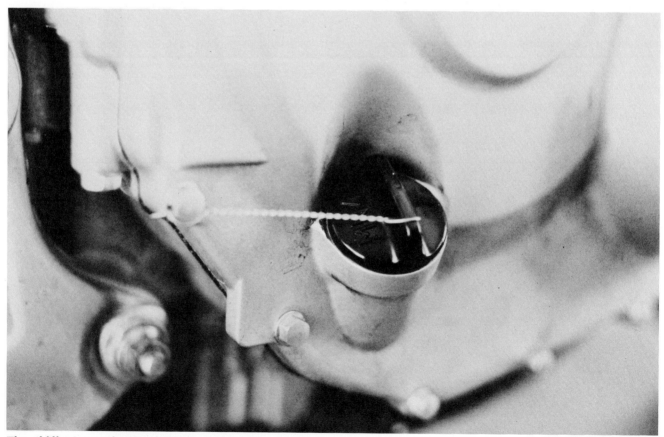

The oil filler cap on this Honda Hurricane has been properly wired. The wire is pulling toward the rotation of the filler cap.

Drilling a series of bolt heads on a Bridgeport mill.

Medium grade Loctite, such as 242, is a good all-around product for fasteners that may be prone to coming loose on a motorcycle. There are many other grades of Loctite for other securing applications. Bearing supply houses usually sell the complete line of Loctite products and can supply data sheets on all Loctite grades and applications.

Chapter 11

Paint and graphics

Once all the performance modifications are done, it is nice to think about how to present the package. The motorcycle market has done some nice packaging in the form of paint and graphics. In fact, in some cases it's really difficult to improve on the manufacturer's work without taking away the attractiveness and identity of the motorcycle. I own two Honda VF1000F Interceptors. I have stared at them for hours trying to come up with a paint scheme that would enhance them, but I have not been successful so I have chosen to leave them alone.

This spray gun is a DeVilbiss model EGA-502. This gun is small and easy to handle. It can be used as a spray brush and is also capable of putting out plenty of paint for larger areas.

A few years ago, changing the paint on a new motorcycle was a way to show some individuality. The motorcycles of earlier days came in what I call monotone colors. Any change in the paint would bring them alive. Today it's different. You must be careful when changing the color and graphic scheme in order to make that individual improvement that some of us like to do.

Motorcycle manufacturers use their paint and graphic layouts to identify the vehicle. This was evident in 1979 at Laguna Seca when Eddie Lawson rode away with a Superbike win on a highly modified Kawasaki MK11 with stock-colored bodywork. It was the start of a new trend in identifying a motorcycle with its production paint and graphics. I was so taken by it that I started my next project soon afterward—a highly modified Kawasaki MK11 with stock paint and graphics.

Looking at the starting line-up of any Superbike event, you will see the factory paint and graphics no different from showroom models. Take the Yamaha line in 1987. It is hard to mistake the performance Yamaha line from a distance. You *know* that is a Yamaha coming over the hill or around that turn. The exact model may not be identifiable from a distance, but there's no mistake about it being a Yamaha!

The idea is to paint your Yamaha or whatever model you choose to a point of improving its appearance, and in doing this establish and express your individuality. This can be a challenge.

Planning the changes for a paint scheme can be a simple and fun thing to do, but you must have an overall plan. With a side view picture of the motorcycle to be painted and a few artist supplies, you can spend hours drawing and coloring a multitude of combinations.

Find a good side view photo of the particular motorcycle. Dealer brochures sometimes have great side view shots. Have a photocopy made, maybe even have an enlarged copy made; the bigger the better. Place vellum or tracing paper over the top of the copy and with a pencil trace the outline of the motorcycle. Maintain good detail of the areas that are to be painted. With this outline of the motorcycle take some colored pens and become creative. Make as many color layouts as necessary. It actually becomes fun and you may be surprised at how artistically creative you can be! Besides, this is how the professionals do it.

If you are going all the way with a complete concept for the motorcycle, leathers, boots, gloves and helmet, get some leather color samples from manufacturers so that you can get as close to color-matching the whole outfit as possible. As for designing the best looking leathers, those people can give you just about anything you can come up with for layout.

Once a layout has been decided on it's just a matter of preparing the surfaces and applying the paint. Well, not really! The real work is still ahead.

Over the years I have done model work both in my business and for a hobby. Painting is the final operation to a finished model, and the actual application of the paint is simple. It is the preparation of the model or motorcycle or whatever is to be painted that requires time and hard work. The ability to have patience in preparation is what determines the difference between a good paint job and a beautiful piece of art.

If you want to have someone else do your preparation and paint work, that is OK. With your own idea down on paper and in color, a good painter can take it from there and deliver the finished product. A good painter should also be pleased to work with your design.

You may even consider doing the preparation of the painted parts yourself, as this is the real time-consuming part of the job, and time is money.

Surface preparation

How simple it used to be to repaint a Honda CB750, a Kawasaki Z1 or those new GS Suzukis. There was a tank, not too large, a small tail piece and two small sidecovers. No front and rear fenders to worry about because they were chrome-plated. Stripping the chrome off the fenders and repainting them was a con-

Materials needed include: body filler for large repairs; body putty and rubber applicator or squeegee; a mask or respirator as paint overspray is not healthy to breathe; mixing sticks and paint strainers (these items are sometimes free as a promotional gesture by paint suppliers).

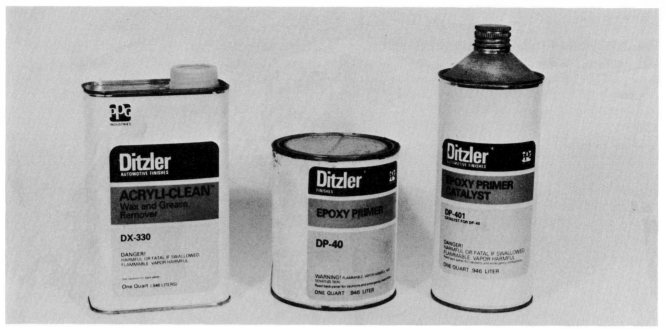

The Ditzler primer is a two-part epoxy. I have used this product for many years with good results on all types of materials: wood, plastic, aluminum and steel. Always use wax and grease remover to clean surfaces to be painted, followed by a good wiping with a clean tack rag just before spraying paint.

sideration. Back then, a repaint was a small task compared to today's sport bikes, whose painted area represents nearly half the area of a small automobile.

Powder coating

Having painted a few motorcycle frames, I am happy to see two things come along: the anodized aluminum frame/swing arm combination and the powder-coating process. Powder coating is a process that coats every little nook and cranny of a steel frame with a uniform thickness of paint. The coating is in powder form as it comes from the spray gun and is electrostatically charged by the gun. The part to be coated is given an opposite charge and attracts the powder coating. The part is uniformly and thoroughly covered, then baked in an oven at 350 to 400 degrees Fahrenheit for fifteen to sixty minutes. The resulting finish is both attractive and extremely durable.

Wheels, triple clamps, fork legs and other parts that need a durable finish can be powder-coated. There are even high-temperature silicon coatings that will withstand exhaust pipe temperatures to 1400 degrees Fahrenheit. Just a word of caution here: the baking temperature may alter the frame alignment.

Companies that do powder coating also provide the cleaning and preparation service. A word of caution here also. Sandblasting with sand that is too heavy does not provide a good surface for powder coating. The results can be an orange-peel finish. A very light sand should be used. Even better is the use of glass beads. I suggest letting the powder-coating company do the whole job.

All bearings must be removed from parts, and any bearing or threaded bosses should be pointed out for masking. The paint can be chased from a threaded hole with a proper tap, but removing powder coating from a precision bearing bore is not a pleasant task, particularly since the bore can be easily masked before coating.

Metal

When preparing a steel or even an aluminum gas tank, I want to see the bare metal. I do not like the idea of those rust worms under the paint work that I am going to spend hours working on. Aluminum does not rust but it can oxidize under paint. In time, blisters will appear under the paint and in order to overcome this the tank must be stripped and re-prepped for painting.

Steel

Light sandblasting is a good way to remove the paint from a steel gas tank. Masking the filler cap and fuel pickup opening with several layers of masking tape is a good idea to keep as much sand out of the tank as possible.

A commercial paint stripper is another way of removing old paint. Once the paint is removed the surface should be processed with metal conditioner for steel. Metal-Prep 79 is the one I use. Go by the manufacturer's directions. Then follow with a chemical coating such as Galvaprep SG. This product produces a gray crystalline coating that resists corrosion and provides good paint adhesion. This process also makes a good base for body fillers in the event that some minor dents have to be repaired. Once the repairs have been made, reapply Galvaprep SG on the area of bare metal. The tank is now ready for priming.

Aluminum

The products for aluminum are called Aluma Kleen and Alodine 1201. I use Aluma Kleen to prepare aluminum for welding. Alodine can be used on aluminum surfaces alone or for priming. I use it on aluminum parts instead of paying the price for anodizing. It is not as long lasting as the anodized finish but it's much less expensive and it gives a pleasant light gold tone to the part.

Products for metal prepping can be purchased at any good auto paint supply store. Please be aware that these products can be hazardous, so read and follow the instructions regarding their use and handling.

Plastic

Most motorcycle bodywork today is made of a thermoforming plastic called ABS. Thermoforming plastics when worked properly produce a relatively strong part with good detail. I did not say a cheap part, however, as anyone knows who has had to replace some of that plastic bodywork. If some of the parts are not too badly damaged there is a process for welding and filling them. The tools for these repairs were developed in Germany, and there are body repair shops around that can offer the service. Even if the body parts have pieces broken off they can be repaired and at considerable savings.

The graphics found on these plastic body parts are usually plastic stick-ons that have been clear-coated over. Some are not clear-coated and simply can be peeled off by applying a little heat with a heat gun or hair dryer. Do not get carried away with the heat, however, as it can distort the body work. Remember, it was formed with heat. If some adhesive is left on the part, the use of mineral spirits or even gasoline on a clean rag will remove it. To remove graphics that have been clear-coated, use sandpaper to remove the clearcoat, then peel off the graphic. Use 60-grit sandpaper.

When preparing plastic bodywork for painting it is not necessary to remove all the old paint; in fact, in this case it makes a good undercoat for the new paint. A complete sanding of all surfaces will be needed, however. Any paint lines should be feathered out to two to three inches. Use 400-grit wet and dry sandpaper with lots of water. A little liquid dishwashing detergent in the water will keep the sandpaper from loading.

After a complete sanding, any small nicks or scratches should be taken care of with a two-part body filler. When using body putty, remember it is used to fill tiny areas, areas that would not be filled in by primer. Use this product sparingly.

Undercoating

Undercoating, or primers as they are called, come in three types: primers, primer-surfacers and primer-sealers.

Primers are for the preparation of a bare surface for accepting and holding the subsequent coats. The

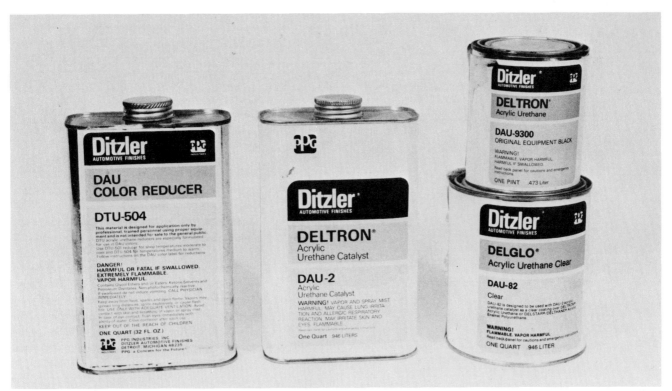

Two-part paints require mixing a catalyst and thinning with the proper reducer. I have found that mixing to the manufacturer's specifications will give the best results. Mixed paint has a reasonable shelf life and if kept cool can be reused for quite a few hours. Check paint specifications.

purpose is to provide maximum adhesion and a corrosion-resistant foundation for the paint that follows. Primers should be applied properly and do not need sanding.

Primer-surfacers contain a high level of pigment solids for filling sand scratches and other minor imperfections. Primer-surfacers can and should be sanded before application of the topcoat.

Primer-sealers will provide the same protection as primers with the added advantage of giving good uniform color holdout for the topcoat. Primer-sealers do not allow the topcoat to soak in as much as primers do, thereby giving a glossier finish. Most primer-sealers do not require sanding before the application of the topcoat.

The ultimate surface preparation would be to use primer for adhesion, followed by primer-surfacer for filling and leveling, followed by a primer-sealer for topcoat holdout. The result is a three-part undercoated surface.

With the cost of materials these days, a three-part primer system seems a bit much, so I use D-P-40, an epoxy primer by Ditzler. It is a two-part epoxy primer that applies well and has great adhesion. It sands nicely and is an excellent base for the topcoat, either enamel or lacquer.

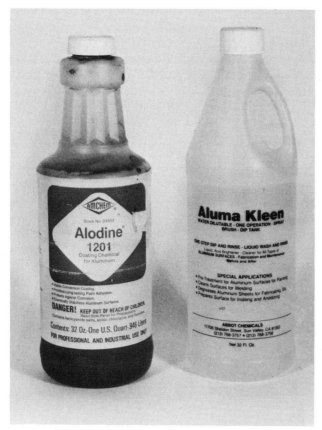

Products used for prepping aluminum. Aluma Kleen can also be used for etching aluminum prior to welding. Alodine is an aluminum coating that is used under paint or as a coating by itself.

Masking techniques

After deciding on the color and layout for the new paint scheme, and after preparation and priming is done, it will be time to mask before painting. Use plenty of tape. It's not expensive and it may be difficult to get that line straight or that curve just right the first time. I prefer to paint the small color areas first. When the tape is removed and the paint has set, then that painted area can be masked again for the adjacent color. Masking tape should be removed before the paint is too dry so that a good clean mask is obtained. To get a really clean mask, use some vinyl masking tape and then just before applying the color, seal the tape with some acrylic clear. This will stop the basecoat from bleeding through.

I don't like to apply an accent color over the main color because it is stacking one layer of paint on another, leaving a build-up at the mask line. When the whole multicolored basecoat is done separately, the paint remains level at the mask line. Before the clearcoat is applied, the paint joints are sanded smooth with 400- or 600-grit wet and dry sandpaper so that when the clearcoat is applied the surface will be level at the paint lines. This requires more work, but it is truly one of the marks of a good paint job, and to me is worth the extra time.

Basecoat/clearcoat systems

Basecoat, or colorcoat as it used to be known, is now a two-part system. The color is applied with two to three coats of acrylic color and then sprayed with an acrylic clearcoat mixed with a urethane catalyst. This system gives a deep, attractive and durable finish. It is also the fastest and easiest system that I have ever used.

Painting is one of those things I really like to do, but I don't get to do it all the time. When I do have a project that requires painting I will practice before painting the actual part. I have always saved one-pound coffee cans which make great practice subjects besides being good for mixing paint and primers. Try some coffee-can painting for practice. I guarantee if you can make that round, convoluted surface look good, then you can make a motorcycle look great!

The spray gun and equipment

A spray gun will be needed for applying paints, although a large and expensive spray gun is not really necessary. I have never owned anything other than a DeVilbiss spray brush. Model EGA-502. This model is small but it can put out a lot of paint or a little paint. There are various sizes of spray nozzles and needles for patterns that range from small to large.

Probably more important than the size of the spray gun is the size of the air source. It is important to have adequate air pressure at the gun in order to atomize the paint properly. Paint manufacturers specify in all cases, from primers to basecoats to topcoats, the proper air pressure at the gun. I find this rule something that is overlooked by many people who are attempting to do their own paint work. Therefore it is absolutely necessary to have an air compressor that is capable of consistently putting out about 60 psi of air.

An air-pressure regulator with a water/oil separator will also be needed inline between the compressor and spray gun. At the spray gun should be a smaller regulator for adjusting that all-important air pressure at the gun. I have an air hose that I use only for painting. An air hose that is used for air tools or an air nozzle can become contaminated and this contamination will end up in your paint job!

Wax and grease remover

Keeping the work surfaces clean during the painting process is important. Use dishwashing detergent and water to wash the surfaces before applying primer or paint. After drying, use a good wax and grease remover. When that dries use what is called a tack rag. This is a piece of cheesecloth that has been treated with a sticky substance which will remove dust and lint. Use this just before applying paint. Avoid touching surfaces to be painted with your hands, as hands are oily and paint does not adhere well to oily surfaces. These items are available from auto paint supply stores.

Basecoat or color coat

Spraying on the basecoat or color coat is the next to last operation. If more than one color is to be used then the area to be painted must be masked and the remaining area covered so that no paint will touch it. To get a good sharp paint line try sealing the masking tape with a thin coat of clear. Spray several coats of color for good coverage. Let the color coat dry a little before removing the masking tape. The right timing for removing the masking tape is something that a feel for must be developed. Too soon and the paint will string. Too late and there is a risk of chipping the paint when the tape's backing is removed.

When the last color coat is good and dry the edges of the mask can be taken down with some 400-grit wet and dry sandpaper. There is always a little more paint build-up at the masking tape. Tape the paint line and mask for the application of the next and adjacent color. Repeat all operations until all colors are applied.

After all the colors have cured it will be time to color sand the surface and repair any spots that have been caused by dust and debris.

Clearcoating

Clean the color surface with a tack rag before spraying the clearcoat. Work in a well-ventilated environment at all times. This last operation should be done in a clean, dust-free situation. Wetting the floor of the work area is a good idea.

Spray the desired amount of clearcoat and let it cure well.

Compounding

When the clearcoat has cured inspect the surfaces for spots that might be a little too big to remove with rubbing compound. Use 600-grit wet and dry sandpaper with water and a little dishwashing soap. Sand just enough to flatten the imperfections. If the clearcoat is sanded through to color it will have to be spotted with more clearcoat and allowed to cure before continuing.

There are two types of compounds. One is for use with a buffer and the other for use by hand; use the hand type and be careful. A lot of paint can be removed with rubbing compound. Use compounds recommended by the paint manufacturer.

Waxing

Let the paint cure for a week or two before applying wax. This will also give enough time for any problem areas to show. If some reworking is necessary it will be better done on a wax-free surface.

When it comes to a brand of wax, you are on your own. There are many good waxes on the market. I use Meguiar's Mirror Glaze number 6.

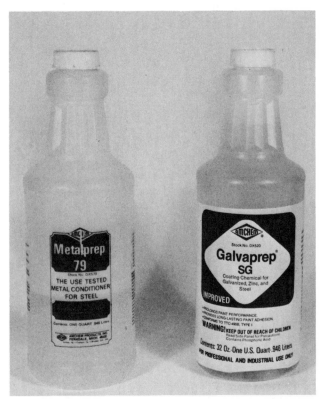

These two products are used for cleaning and coating steel before painting.

Chapter 12

The checkered flag

The end of the racing season is a checkered flag, a time to look at what's left of the motorcycle, rider and the racing program. Several questions arise. Shall we do it again next year? How will we afford a new motorcycle? Who's going to pay for spares?

Answers arise, too. Well, maybe this set of leathers is good for one more year. Replace fifth gear and the gearbox will be as good as new. The van won't make it to another race, but that's OK because JR got a new Ford and we will use his. We got the number one plate—that will get us some sponsorship. Of course we're going racing!

In Southern California where I'm from, there isn't that much time between the end of one racing season and the start of the next season. I can't remember when I haven't taken a little motorcycle ride on Christmas Day. Mind you, I'm not knocking it but I sort of envy people in Colorado or Minnesota or Maine who have had their motorcycles in storage for three or four months when suddenly spring is here and the motorcycles can be taken for a ride. Now that first spring ride has got to be really exciting, something you don't experience if you can go for a ride or racing almost every weekend of the year! If I don't get a motorcycle fix for several weeks I can hardly stand to be around myself.

This book, in part, is about my involvement with motorcycles and motorcycle people—both on the street and at the races—over the last twenty years. The motorcycle is just the medium for what is really important to the sport: the people. This project is really about the people whom I have come to know over the years.

Many of the photos in this book are about the preparation of a Suzuki GSXR750 owned, built and ridden by Jeff Stern of Woodland Hills, California. This project was supported in more ways than one by the George and Pat Stern Racing and Rehabilitation Foundation—that's Mom and Dad! Jeff Stern works as a motorcycle mechanic at a Simi Valley, California,

Suzuki dealership. Then there is Paula, Jeff's girlfriend, without whom there would be no lap times sheets, no pit board signals, no potato chips, no beer and no one for Jeff to throw over his shoulder after a fast lap.

Then there's Jeff Rheaume, a friend, racer, jump-in-and-help-anytime worker and co-rider in endurance events. Supporters like Ben Kaufman show up along with Dwight, Joe and Rollin. I show up about noon. I was just going for a short Sunday ride when I got lost and ended up at the racetrack. They greet me by saying, "Hey look, Mentor is here." With people like that gathered together, of course we're going racing again next year.

The group of people that I just described are real, but they are not the only ones. If you were to walk into the pit area of any track in the country on race day, every pit would have a group there just like ours. Only the names and faces are different. Well, maybe they race one of those "other" brands of motorcycles.

There are different levels of involvement in this motorcycle sport. When I went racing on my 50 cc Kreidler, I knew that I would never be a Kenny Roberts. But I don't think the feelings that I experienced when I won a local club race were any different than those Kenny felt winning a Grand Prix. I'm sure that when I crashed, the pain I experienced was no different than the pain Kenny Roberts experienced when he crashed. When I won a season championship at the local club level, the feelings were the same as well—if only it had been a world championship event! I even won some money once: $100. It might just as well have been a million. The feelings were the same.

When I think of my involvement in motorcycling and motorcycle racing I recall the story about the pig and the chicken, and their involvement in the traditional ham and egg breakfast. I have to go with the pig. The chicken is merely a participant in the event, but the pig is committed, WFO!

Sources

Living in Southern California is in some respects like living in the center of the universe when it comes to the availability of motorcycle parts and products. With the help of United Parcel Service, I can get just about anything by the next working day.

Here is a list of some top-notch suppliers that may supply you with parts for your motorcycle project. Even as close as I am to suppliers, I still can't resist a good catalog; I have them all. Catalogs help keep me in touch with the motorcycle world.

Storz Performance Accessories
1362 Tower Square #2
Ventura, CA 93003
Former Harley-Davidson dirt track tuner Steve Storz has always catered to the dirt tracker. In recent years he also has turned to helping the street rider and road racer by supplying items such as Ceriani forks, steering dampers, Grimeca calipers and mounting components. Storz is also the innovator and supplier of Superbike bar mounts. The catalog is filled with many more performance motorcycle products.

Lockhart Motorcycle Products
991 Calle Negocio Street
San Clemente, CA 92672
The catalog is a work of art and also lists some outstanding items. Based on their successful endurance racing team, Lockhart has a good feel for the needs of street rider and road racer.

Earl's Performance Products
825 East Sepulveda
Carson, CA 90745
Performance plumbing components for brake lines, oil lines and other hard-to-find performance hardware.

Megacycle Cams
90 Mitchell Boulevard
San Rafael, CA 94903

Web-Cam
1663 Superior Avenue
Costa Mesa, CA 92627

Vance & Hines
14010 Marquardt Avenue
Santa Fe Springs, CA 90670
Basically a drag-racing-oriented facility, the firm still provides a number of quality items for street and road race applications.

Yoshimura R&D of America
4555 Carter Court
Chino, CA 91710
Serious racers have depended on Yoshimura performance products for years.

Toomey Racing USA
3034 Propeller Drive
Paso Robles, CA 93446
Among other things, Toomey has the best wheel truing stand on the market.

Mikuni American Corporation
8910 Mikuni Avenue
Northridge, CA 91324
A good source for technical data on carburetion.

Sudco Mikuni
1824 East 22nd Street
Los Angeles, CA 90058
These people handle a lot of items too numerous to mention. Order the catalog first.

Kosman Specialties
340 Fell Street
San Francisco, CA 94102
Lockheed calipers.

Aircraft Spruce & Speciality Co
201 West Truslow Avenue
Fullerton, CA 92632

This company is known as *the* supplier for the home-built aircraft enthusiast but it is also one of the best sources for small orders of 4130 chromoly tubing and plate stock, a difficult item to buy in small quantities. Also a supplier of aircraft-quality fasteners. The catalog is worth the effort.

International Aviation Publishers
PO Box 36 1000 College View Drive
Riverton, WY 82501

Publishers of *Standard Aviation Maintenance Handbook*, a great book to have. Filled with information dealing with the sport of flying and maintenance of aircraft, much of the information can be applied to the sport of motorcycling.

Mitutoyo
16925 Gale Avenue
City of Industry, CA 91745

Possibly the best source for high-quality precision measuring instruments, micrometer, dial indicators, bore gauges and so on.

Simons Ohlins
2570 Leghorn Street
Mountain View, CA 94043

Carrillo Industries
33041 Calle Perfecto
San Juan Capistrano, CA 92675

Manufacturers of high-quality chromoly connecting rods.

Slater Bros.
PO Box 1
Mica, WA 99023

Brembo calipers and components. Marvic and Tecnomagnesio racing wheels.

Barnett
PO Box 2826
Santa Fe Springs, CA 90670

Manufacturers of high-performance clutch components.

Index